Wonders at the Veil

Wonders at The Veil

Creating a Living Relationship
with Your Loved Ones
Who Have Died

Lynn Rollins Stull

Institute for Veil Work

Design by Meadowlark Publishing Services.

Cover painting by Lynn Rollins Stull.
Photos courtesy of the author.
Illustrations in chapter 16 by Marjorie Spock, from *Eurythmy*, Anthroposophic Press.

Published by Institute for Veil Work.
www.lynnstull.com

Manufactured in the United States of America.
ISBN 978-0-9974576-0-5

Published 2016.

Lara Stull, I love you.

Human freedom may choose whether or not
to seek and maintain a conscious relationship
with the dead. Nothing, either from within
or from without, compels it.
It is a deed of purest love.
—Albert Steffen

Contents

Contents

Part 1

Orientation

Welcome to *Wonders at the Veil*, the book that invites you to the practice of "veil work." Veil work is a very special spiritual practice that is little written about today—a main motivation for me to write this book. It is such important work, vital for spiritual healing in our scattered, disconnected modern world. Veil work has proven valuable beyond measure in my own life, and I offer this book to encourage you to consider creating a practice of your own. If you do, I am confident you will find it rewarding, heart opening—and wondrous!

Part 1 consists of two chapters. Chapter 1, An Introduction to Veil Work, presents an overview of the practice and answers some basic questions about it. In chapter 2, Spiritual Evolution and Reincarnation, we will look at these two spiritual realities that underlie the work.

1

An Introduction To Veil Work

I am very honored to introduce you to an extraordinary spiritual practice, one that you have probably never considered and may not have even heard of before. In *Wonders at the Veil,* you will discover what I call veil work. In veil work, we intentionally approach the veil between the physical and spiritual worlds for two specific purposes: to be of service to our loved ones who have died and to remain in relationship with them—a living relationship.

Wonders at the Veil, which is deeply rooted in the extraordinary work of Rudolf Steiner (1861–1925), will teach you ways to penetrate the veil between the living and the dead. You will learn techniques to communicate with loved ones you thought had traveled beyond your reach. Through selfless service, you will reconnect with the people you loved while they were alive, and your practice will truly help and support them as they journey in the spiritual realms.

Does reconnecting with your loved ones in the spiritual world seem impossible to you? It *is* possible. I have made a commitment to veil work for the past eighteen years, and I have found it life

---

*Does reconnecting with your loved ones
in the spiritual world seem impossible to you?
It is possible.*

---

changing—transformative on every level. I am confident that if you commit to this practice, you will not only serve your loved ones, but you will nourish your own spiritual growth immeasurably. And while it may seem paradoxical at first, serving the dead will actually make you feel more alive than ever before. Your heart will expand and your whole life will become a larger vessel, able to hold more love and joy. You will have the great satisfaction of supporting the people with whom you once shared this physical life—and they will eagerly welcome your renewed connection. Your practice will have ripple effects too: positive impacts beyond the ones you and your loved ones directly experience.

In uncovering your own unique wonders at the veil, you will be doing research at the frontiers of spiritual exploration, at the leading edge of a unique movement that seeks to serve humanity as a whole—on both sides of the veil. As you join others in blazing this trail, your veil practice will serve to further humanity's collective spiritual growth, helping create a more loving and soul-filled world for everyone. This is the promise—and the reality—of veil work.

My Path to the Veil

In the spring of 1997 my daughter, Lara, died in my arms on the way to the hospital. She was eight and a half years old. After Lara's death, I was moved to approach the veil for three reasons. First, I had become a student of Rudolf Steiner's work, and based on my studies I understood that it was possible for me to provide Lara with spiritual nourishment even though she was now in the spiritual world. Second, I knew that it would allow me to continue to build a relationship with her that would feel true and alive despite the fact that her death had physically separated us. Finally, I wanted to better understand where she was now that she had left her body: What new world had she entered? What was it like for her to be there? What was she doing, and how was she faring?

Meeting Rudolf Steiner

I was introduced to the writings of Rudolf Steiner just six months before Lara died. He was the one who first opened my eyes to the possibility of penetrating the veil, and I still find his work the most detailed, meaningful, and illuminating on the subject.

I had gone to a bookstore to research educational options for Lara, who faced physical disabilities that made finding the right school a challenge. I had heard about Waldorf Schools, which teach based on a system Steiner created, and I was considering that option. As it happened, the bookstore I visited that day had only one of his books in stock, and it had nothing to do with his system of education: it was called *How to Know Higher Worlds*.

By "higher worlds," Steiner was referring to the spiritual realms beyond this physical world. They have been a lifelong interest of mine, so I was immediately attracted to the book and read it with great interest. Then I learned that there was a bookshop and library nearby that was wholly devoted to Steiner's works. It was a friendly volunteer at this bookshop who informed me that Steiner spoke a lot about working with the dead.

If Steiner is new to you and this book inspires you to investigate further, you will find that his writings are vast, encompassing topics as diverse as agricultural methods, architecture, literary criticism, the arts, and medicine. But it was his exploration of what he termed "spiritual science" that captured my imagination and led me to the

---

*The opportunity to reconnect with someone you
thought you had lost truly is a wonder!*

---

veil. Steiner offers a unique and disciplined approach to building
relationships with those who have died. It is very objective, in
the sense that it is based on his direct experience of the spiritual
realms—worlds he explored himself through a dedicated practice
of spiritual exercises and meditations. Thus his approach is free of
sentimentality, leading instead to an experience of deep, devotional
love and wisdom. I feel very blessed that Steiner lectured extensively
on this topic and that his lectures have been published in many
books, and I still rely on his work as I continue to develop my
practice.

Why Veil Work?

Now you know something of what veil work entails: intentionally
exploring the boundaries between the physical and spiritual worlds
and building relationships with those on the other side. And I
have told you something of how I came to this practice. But why
should you invest your time and energy in veil work? There are
several reasons why it is an important practice to consider adopting
as your own.

First, let's look at it on a personal level. The opportunity to
reconnect with someone you thought you had lost truly is a *wonder!*
It is simply astonishing to learn that the "wall" that separates you
from your loved one is not solid at all but is actually porous—and
growing thinner in our time. You *can* reestablish a connection: a
very different one from the connection you shared while you both
lived, certainly, but an intimate one nonetheless.

If you are grieving a loved one's passing, veil work acts as a balm you can apply at any time to receive comfort. Grieving is a process that never truly has an end point, as it resurfaces and changes in quality over time. But wherever you are in the process, veil work can soothe your heart and lift your spirit.

Also on a personal level, the practice offers endless opportunities for spiritual growth. As you will soon learn, communication flows in both directions through the veil, and your loved ones are eager to guide and support you even as you commit to serving them through your practice. The results can be surprising! You may be struck with a sudden inspiration, a thought or image that you are sure is not your own but that changes the trajectory of your day—or your life. You may find yourself led into studies or activities that you never considered before and that bring you joy and deepen your sense of wonder. Over my years of veil work practice, this has happened to me again and again, and in this book I will share some of the ways this has manifested for me.

Moving outward now from your own experience and toward your family and friends and the communities where you live and work, you will find that, ultimately, veil work affects everyone you come into contact with. As you develop spiritually through your practice, your knowledge and perception will broaden, and the choices you make and the ways in which you interact with others will undergo a series of shifts for the better. While perfection eludes all of us in the physical world, you will find you are increasingly able to live according to the universal principles of Truth, Beauty, and Goodness, essential qualities of a spiritual life that will guide your service.

The effects of your practice will ripple outward on the other side of the veil as well. When communication between you and your loved ones is flowing freely, a kind of symmetry of movement takes place between the physical and spiritual worlds, with spiritual evolution quickening on both sides. The support and nourishment you offer to your loved ones is reflected into their surroundings

*Spiritual connection and evolution
are the remedies to disconnection.*

and to other souls and spiritual beings in those realms. This is one of the most powerful effects of veil work: you have the ability to make a meaningful contribution to the evolution of all. Fundamentally, the cycle of birth and death—experiencing, learning, and spiritually growing through lifetimes in *both* the physical and spiritual worlds—is the process that allows us to move toward becoming Divine human beings, truly made in the likeness of God, the original Creator of all life. Through veil work, you consciously become an active participant in that forward motion.

Finally, as I touched on earlier, veil work offers unique opportunities for frontier spiritual research. As you engage in the practices and note your experiences in a journal that you will create for this purpose, you will add to our collective wisdom about the nature of the veil and how we can move across it to help and support one another on both sides. You will be forging and widening a path that others may then travel more easily.

I am laying markers on the path myself as I experiment with the principles I learned from Rudolf Steiner and adapt them to my own life and practice. Through this book, I am describing the path as I know it. But I am just one soul, and there is a universe of experience to explore. I wrote this book in the hopes that it will lead many others to the practice, and that each person will develop their own unique tributaries to the path and freely share their experience. That way, we can teach and guide one another and quickly develop our knowledge and practical communication techniques. It is important that we get many new shoulders to the wheel as soon as we can, as I believe this is a matter of great urgency.

Why Now?

Why practice veil work now? You need only look to your own experience of the world around you for the answer to this question. It is important to do veil work now because we live in a world that is plagued by disconnection from spirit. Our disconnected state injures us personally, breeds violence, and harms the planet that we all love. *Spiritual connection and evolution are the remedies to disconnection,* and if it is in our power to hasten them, this is something we must do. Spiritual evolution is not just some pretty thing we aspire to so we can consider ourselves "good" people. It is an absolute necessity for the survival of our world. When we nurture spiritual evolution on both sides of the veil, we are working in all the realms where it needs to take place, and we can heal the illness of disconnection more actively and effectively than we can by working solely on our own evolution on this side of the veil.

Here is another reason why now is the time: extraordinary opportunities exist as a result of our spiritual evolution to date. As Steiner writes, "Today there are souls who feel, even if out of the deepest recesses of their instincts, that they wish to experience something of the spiritual world! They are the pioneers of a future when souls will come who will consider it important to cultivate a spiritual life founded on the cognition of the spiritual worlds."[1] Barbara Marx Hubbard, a leader of conscious evolution, states, "We are a future-oriented family of humanity who sense within ourselves the birth of the Universal Human."[2]

Even as human societies have become increasingly materialistic, the veil between the physical and spiritual worlds has thinned. A recent Pew Research Center survey disclosed that 29 percent of Americans have "felt in touch with someone who has died."[3] Also, our spiritual capacities have increased as a result of the development of our chakras, the spiritual organs of the body. Just as we use our physical sense organs like our eyes, ears, and nose to perceive and understand the physical world, chakras allow us to perceive and understand the spiritual world. If you are unfamiliar with chakras, they are specific points in the subtle energy body, primarily located in the general area along the spine from the sacrum to the crown of the head. These spiritual organs are still evolving and can be strengthened and developed through spiritual disciplines, including meditation. Steiner writes, "The further we advance in soul development, the more regularly structured our soul organism [chakra system] becomes."[4]

I believe that eventually our spiritual organs will evolve to the point where we can regularly and openly communicate with our loved ones who have died, and it will feel like the most natural thing in the world. We can bring "eventually" closer to the present by practicing veil work *now*.

Who This Book Is For

Veil work is for anyone who is drawn to the benefits I have outlined. If you are grieving a loss, my hope is that veil work will bring you comfort. Often with the death of a loved one comes a feeling of loss of control. Veil work is something proactive you can do that will give you a feeling of being enveloped in grace and warmth. If you feel devoted to your loved one's well-being and want to help them navigate the spiritual realms and find sustenance there, veil work offers practical ways to put that desire into action. And if you find the prospect of doing research at the spiritual frontier as exciting as I do, veil work offers an uncharted landscape that is just waiting to be explored.

You may be drawn to veil work for a very different reason—you have already been contacted by a deceased loved one. Remember: the veil is a two-way street, and souls on both sides can decide to reach out. Perhaps someone came to you in a dream and told you something significant: a message that shifted your thinking, how you felt, or even the course of your life. Maybe you distinctly heard your loved one's voice calling out a warning or asking you an important question or pointing out an opportunity. Or an object that reminds you of your loved one keeps showing up in your surroundings, or an aroma you associate with them, or a piece of music, or even a word or a number. You have been contacted in ways such as these, and now you're thinking, *Okay, what am I supposed to do with this?* If this has happened to you, you can be sure that your loved one is very eagerly awaiting contact. When you set up a formal practice, instead of having such experiences at seemingly random times, you will learn how to make *deliberate* contact, and you will gain experience in interpreting the communications you receive in return.

Yes, But ... Resistances to Veil Work

For most people, contemplating a veil work practice requires a radical shift in thinking: *Wait ... something I thought was impossible is something I can actually do?* It can take some time to catch up to that idea. Contemplating the practice might also bring up fear, which you can recognize in the form of resistance.

Let's get the obvious out of the way first: that voice inside you that might be saying, *Talk to dead people? But that's crazy! Everyone will think I'm nuts. I will think I'm nuts!*

That is the voice of your twenty-first-century culture speaking—the one that values the material and scientific above all else and considers all metaphysical experience illegitimate, mere figments of the imagination. But consider this: when you enter into communication with your loved ones who have died, you are continuing a cross-cultural tradition that dates back thousands of years. Veil work is simply a form of practice that happens to be taking place now, at a time in human history when the veil is thinning—a time of prime opportunity for this work.

A Sampling of Traditions:
Welcoming In the Dead

People have found ways to connect with their deceased loved ones cross-culturally through history. Many of these practices are categorized broadly as "ancestor worship." In many cases, however, "worship" does not seem like an accurate description of what is going on. In the Shinto religion of Japan, for example, four occasions during the year are set aside to honor family members who have died: one at the new year, one each at the vernal and autumnal equinoxes, and Obon, the Festival of the Dead, in summer. During, Obon, the dead are "welcomed back to the house and given a feast by members of the family." This does not seem like "worship" so much as a festive family celebration—to which their deceased loved ones are invited! There is also a Shinto practice of reading to the recently dead; every seven days for the first forty-nine days after a person dies, family members make special offerings and read sutras (sacred scriptures) to them. More casual contact is also common as individuals ask their deceased loved ones for assistance and seek their advice.[5]

In sub-Saharan Africa cultures, deceased family members are also honored, and people see them as continuing to "take an interest in the living world."[6] In Hindu tradition, people make ritual offerings of food to their loved ones who have died, believing "it reminds the ancestors' spirits that they are not forgotten and are loved, so it brings them peace."[7] And deep in the history of Catholic tradition we find the practice of offering prayers, called acclamatory, to the dead, including "wishes of peace, the good (i.e. eternal salvation), light, refreshment, life, eternal life, union with God, with Christ, and with the angels and saints."[8]

These are just a few examples of the creative ways people of different cultures have, through ritual and dedicated practice, intentionally retained a connection with their loved ones who

When you enter into communication with your loved ones who have died, you are continuing a cross-cultural tradition that dates back thousands of years.

have died. It is not at all unusual and is in fact a time-honored practice worldwide.

Fear of Death—and the Words *Death, Died, Dead*

Now let's confront another obstacle: our contemporary avoidance of the whole idea of death, even to the point of refusing to utter the word *death*.

Until very recently in the human history of the West, an intimate experience of death was commonplace. Extended families lived together, young and old alike, and people did not die in hospitals or nursing homes; they died at home, cared for by family and friends until the last breath, with every hour of the process a communal experience. With death such a familiar part of life, people did not tiptoe around the loss. They grieved as we all do when we lose a loved one's physical presence, but they did not avoid clearly stating what had happened or pretend there was some way to soften the fact of it. Consider what we might say today: "She has passed away (or over, or on)." And we might hasten to add something like "but she lives on in our hearts."

It is actually simpler than that: *she died.* She ceased to exist on Earth. The physical body, the bodily sheath that housed her spirit and soul, died and will decompose according to the physical laws of the Earth plane. Doing veil work requires accepting the reality of death and being willing and able to talk about it honestly. And to do that, we need to get comfortable with using the words that accurately name what has occurred.

Fear of the Dead

Most of us grew up with ghost stories: tales of hauntings by malevo-lent spirits, sometimes missing limbs or even heads, perhaps told around the campfire or in a candlelit room for the express purpose of scaring the daylights out of us. Horror films, the haunted house on Halloween, the seer with supernatural powers leading the séance, the Ouija board moving of its own accord—all of these things can give us a cellular memory of fear in connection with the dead. If these old feelings come up as you contemplate undertaking a veil work practice, be patient with yourself. Take a moment to appreci-ate just how effectively you were indoctrinated with these scary thoughts and images—and then set them aside. As you develop and grow in your veil work practice, those memories will be supplanted by real, authentic experiences of joy and delight and, yes, wonder. You will be able to see for yourself just how irrelevant those made-up tales of hauntings are.

I do recognize that when some human beings die, their soul and spirit seem to be caught or stuck in the soul world (a realm of the spiritual world you will learn more about in chapter 17) rather than moving on to the pure land of spirit. But this is not my area of expertise, nor have I had any encounters with these beings. Also, I am not saying there is no such thing as malevolence in the spiritual world, with impacts in both the spiritual and physical worlds. When you consider reincarnation, which we will discuss in the next chapter, and the state of the world around you, it stands to reason that there must be negative influences on both sides of the veil. However, you can protect yourself and your loved ones from harm, and I will teach you how to ensure that you stay healthy and safe as you do your practice.

Fear of Grief

Another source of resistance is the fear of uncovering old wounds. You may be concerned that if you make contact with your loved one again, the most acute feelings of sadness you experienced immediately following their death will resurface and you will suffer pain. I will not promise you that this will not happen, but I will say that if intense grief resurfaces, it will be an authentic experience that is part of a life fully lived. It will also be balanced by the comfort and healing that come with reconnection. For me, grief never goes away; it still arises, unpredictably and for varying lengths of time. But I have also found that because I do veil work I have many more moments of joy and creativity than I would have otherwise, and my capacity to foster the virtues of Truth, Beauty, and Goodness in my life and the world around me have greatly increased. When I feel connection with my loved one, my heart warms. I will always prefer that my daughter were still alive in a physical healthy body, yet I have found a new way to be in relationship with her and others in a very deep sense that is both *living* and real.

Painful Relationships

Finally in the list of resistances to veil work, there is the fact that your relationship with your loved one who has died was not perfect, and you may resist revisiting its imperfections. You may not have been the perfect wife, father, sister, or friend. You may have said and done some things that you regret and would prefer not to think about again. We can mend our errors and heal our wounds through consciously serving and co-creating with our loved ones.

---

*We can mend our errors and heal our wounds
through consciously serving and co-creating
with our loved ones.*

Loved ones who have died cannot change circumstances once they enter the spiritual world, but we can help them. As you will learn later in the book, your loved ones spend some of their time in the spiritual realms reviewing their own impacts on the people they knew when they were living, for good and bad. And as part of that they may examine some things that took place between the two of you. You can help alleviate your loved one's pain regarding times when either of you were less than loving to the other. But for now I recommend focusing on regaining a healthy connection by creating a strong spiritual foundation, the framework that will serve your new relationship. That will offer limitless opportunities for positive interaction that nourishes and heals you both.

Moving Ahead: How to Use This Book

Now that we have looked at veil work in broad strokes, let us take a preview of how to cultivate a veil work practice. I have designed this book to take you step by step through the practice. I encourage you to read the chapters in order. If you are someone who just does not read that way and prefers to dip in here and there or jump to what seems like the most interesting chapter first, I would simply ask that you make sure to read the entire book before you are through, as all of it is intended to support you in developing and sustaining your practice.

Each chapter is designed to provide you with content on a specific aspect of veil work. Then, at the end of each chapter you will find activities to support you in deepening your understanding of the content.

Here in chapter 1 of part 1: An Introduction to Veil Work, I have given you an overview of what veil work is, why it is important, who can benefit from it, why you might resist it, and considerations for moving past resistance. Chapter 2 further orients you by looking at the nature of spiritual evolution and reincarnation, emphasizing that spiritual growth takes place both during and between incarnations.

Next, in part 2: Preparation, you will begin setting the stage for your veil work practice. First you will define the intention of your practice, the subject of chapter 3. In chapter 4 you will create a journal that will both support and document your work. Chapter 5 offers suggestions, based on my own experience, for setting up a successful practice.

Part 3: Communication Basics is all about creating the best possible environment for communicating through the veil and discovering some ways this communication is likely to take place. In chapter 6 you will learn how to create a mood that is conducive to exploring the veil. Chapters 7 and 8 address effective communication techniques—with one chapter devoted to ways to reach out to the other side and the other to receiving communication.

Then it will be time to begin your practice in earnest! Part 4: Reading Spirit-Filled Works describes the core practice of veil work. In chapter 9 you will learn why this is the foundation of your service, and chapters 10 and 11 will help you decide which reading materials to choose as well as offer suggestions from my own library.

Then you will start to branch out into other ways to communicate in part 5: Co-Creating Through the Veil. In this part I will give you an overview of co-creating, the subject of chapter 12. Then I will share the ways that I have been led to co-create with my loved ones. Chapter 13 discusses the three spiritual qualities that make intentional co-creation possible: Truth, Beauty, and Goodness. The three chapters that follow all have to do with art.

Chapter 14 offers an overview of art as a spiritual activity. Working with color, as you will learn in chapter 15, offers fruitful sustenance to those in the spiritual world. Promptings from my loved ones across the veil have led me to explore the spiritual dimensions of color—I even became an artist and sold paintings as a result! I will share with you some insights I gained about color along the way. Chapter 16 will introduce you to eurythmy, a form of human movement originated by Rudolf Steiner that the dead can perceive and that is based on the creative and formative power of the sounds of words, tones, and intervals of music. Powerful impulses and strong support I received from my loved ones sent me down a path toward becoming a practitioner of this movement form—a eurythmist. I will offer highlights of both the theory and practice of eurythmy in this chapter.

With your practice now well under way, in part 6: An Imagining of the Soul's Journey, I will introduce you to the realms through which the soul travels after death. This will give you important context for your continued work. Chapter 17 describes the first part of the journey—through the soul realms. In chapter 18 we explore the journey through what Steiner calls "spirit country"—the realm of pure spirit.

Finally, in part 7 I will offer ideas for sustaining the work. Chapter 19 addresses ways to support your practice so you can remain consistent and engaged. I close the book by offering my intention and hopes for you as you continue your practice on your own.

It gives me great joy to share the exciting and inspiring practice of veil work with you. As you begin your work at this spiritual frontier, please know that though your journey will be unique to you and the loved ones you contact, your dedication to this practice will uplift us all—on both sides of the veil. It is time to begin.

Veil Work Activities

Contemplations

Now I invite you to consider the following questions. They are designed to help you start thinking about adopting veil work as your own spiritual practice. You might write your answers down and later either cut and paste them into or rewrite them in the journal you will create in chapter 4.

- Who is the one person in your life who has died that you would particularly like to rekindle a relationship with?
- When you think what it might be like to intentionally communicate with your loved ones who have died, what thoughts or images first come to mind?
- Does your current spiritual path have teachings about approaching the veil between you and your loved ones?
- Had you heard of Rudolf Steiner before I introduced him to you? Do you feel open to exploring Steiner's view of the spiritual world we inhabit after we die?
- What do you imagine that reestablishing your connection with a deceased loved one might feel like?
- If you find the thought of exploring at the veil exciting, what excites you about it? What do you think or hope will happen when you do?
- Describe any reservations or fears you have about embarking on this path.
- Are you grieving the death of a loved one now? If so, how do you think veil work could help ease your grief?
- Did you have a troubled relationship with someone you loved who has died? If so, how do you imagine veil work could help heal the rift between you?
- Have you already been contacted by someone who has died? Briefly describe your experience—what did you see, hear, smell, think, or feel?

2

Spiritual Evolution and Reincarnation

Your practice of serving your loved ones at the veil is part of a much larger picture of humankind's spiritual development and evolution. In this chapter we will explore spiritual evolution and the role of reincarnation, including the idea of reincarnation as a kind of "breathing through the veil" between the physical and spiritual worlds.

Spiritual Evolution

Just as we have evolved on the physical plane—from the Stone Age to our current Digital Revolution—we have also evolved spiritually through consecutive patterns of death and rebirth, known as reincarnation.

The overall pattern of spiritual evolution reveals the human being evolving from a time when, as Steiner writes, we "possessed the faculty of *instinctive* clairvoyance.... Men belonging to that ancient humanity were still able to gaze into the spiritual worlds whence the human being descends into his physical body on the

---

*Now our spiritual task is to lift the veil between us
and the spiritual world and reunite with God.*

Earth" [emphasis mine].[1] Then our individual connection to the spiritual worlds began to be cut off, but we were at least directed by the spiritual worlds via "chosen" leaders who spoke for the Divine—think of the Egyptian pharaohs and Greek oracles. We may not generally have allowed ourselves a direct connection with the Divine during such times, but at least these individuals connected us with the spiritual worlds in some way. Today we experience the evolutionary effects of the materialism of the Scientific and Industrial Revolutions, which taught the supremacy of the human mind over spirit, resulting in many of us feeling separation from the Divine. It is important to note, however, that we needed to be overpowered by materialism to start on the path toward becoming fully individualized as human beings, to take matters into our own hands, and to direct our own spiritual growth. Now our spiritual task, through our own initiative and free will, is to lift the veil between us and the spiritual world and to reunite with God, not through instinctive clairvoyance, but by seeing, nourishing, and strengthening the Divine within ourselves. As Saint Paul says in Ephesians 3:20, "Now to Him who is able to do far more abundantly than all that we ask or think, according to the power at work *within me* [emphasis mine]."

For me, a verse by Rudolf Steiner paints an eloquent picture of our spiritual progression from connection to disconnection and then to a higher state of evolution.

The Stars Spoke Once to Man

The Stars spoke once to Man
It is World Destiny
That they are silent now.
To be aware of the silence
Can become pain for earthly man.

But in the deepening silence
There grows and ripens
What Man speaks to the Stars.
To be aware of the speaking
Can become strength for Spirit-Man.

(Note: Spirit-Man is the individuated human being who
is fully spiritualized.)

If you spend some time with this verse, you will understand that it holds a strong message for veil work. The image of speaking to Stars (the Cosmic Forces) is a way of describing our conscious lifting of the veil between ourselves and the beings that dwell in the spiritual realms. The verse confirms that we are now at a point in our spiritual evolution when we have the spiritual tools to speak to the Stars, and it illuminates the path ahead. To take this message into the depths of our souls gives us fortitude for spiritual striving. And a part of our striving is awakening to the fact that a conscious, intentional practice of veil work is part of our journey toward spiritual evolution.

Reincarnation as a Component of Spiritual Evolution

Reincarnation is the process of the individual's *spirit* incarnating into the physical body (or physical sheath) on Earth, using the *soul* as the intermediary, to learn those lessons we can only experience here in the physical world. Upon death, the individual's spirit and soul leave the sheath and take those experiences into the spiritual world. There, we have the opportunity—according to our level of spiritual development—to refine and develop further as we prepare for another life on Earth. I see the process of reincarnation as a gift you and I have been given: the opportunity to evolve toward becoming "perfect just as your heavenly Father is perfect." (Matthew 5:48) And as we will learn in part 4 on reading spirit-filled works, veil work fits in quite nicely with the process of spiritual evolution and the gift of reincarnation.

Although I grew up Catholic—a religious tradition that does not openly recognize reincarnation—reincarnation has always seemed natural to me. I am not alone in feeling this way. Twenty-four percent of Americans and 22 percent of Christians believe in reincarnation.[2]

Reincarnation Across Spiritual Traditions

Many spiritual and religious traditions, around the world and since ancient times, have accepted reincarnation as fact and have passed their views on how it works through the generations through scripture, storytelling, and scholarship. The Dalai Lama, the spiritual leader of Tibet who as a boy was recognized as a reincarnation of the previous Dalai Lama according to foretold signs, recently spoke to the near universal presence of reincarnation in India:

_Reincarnation is the process of the individual's
spirit incarnating into the physical body
(or physical sheath) on Earth, using the soul
as the intermediary, to learn those lessons
we can only experience here in the physical world._

Sentient beings come to this present life from their previous lives and take rebirth again after death. This kind of continuous rebirth is accepted by all the ancient Indian spiritual traditions and schools of philosophy ...[3]

The Hindu leader Mahatma Gandhi said, "I cannot think of permanent enmity between man and man, and believing as I do in the theory of reincarnation, I live in the hope that if not in this birth, in some other birth I shall be able to hug all of humanity in friendly embrace."[4] And in the Hindu scripture the _Bhagavad Gita_, Krishna proclaims, "The end of birth is death; the end of death is birth: this is ordained!"

What about indigenous cultures? Of North American tribal societies, Gary R. Varner writes, "many have had a belief in Reincarnation."[5]

When it comes to reincarnation and the Bible, one of my favorite sources of information is Edward Reaugh Smith's book _The Soul's Long Journey: How the Bible Reveals Reincarnation_. A successful lawyer and businessman, Smith studied and taught the deeper meanings of the Bible for twenty-five years before discovering Rudolf Steiner's work. Smith cites passages from both the Old and New Testaments as indicators of reincarnation, often citing as well references from Steiner and other Christian writers including

Sylvia Cranston, Ian Stevenson, M.D. and Geddes MacGregor. I have included books by these authors in the Veil Work Activities section at the end of this chapter.

Rudolf Steiner lectured often about reincarnation and also explained why the figures in the Bible didn't speak directly about the subject, maintaining that in each evolutionary time period, spiritual leaders and teachers speak only of what our soul is ready to receive at that time. A favorite Steiner lecture of mine on this subject is included in his book *The Gospel of St. Luke*. In Luke 6:20–23 we have the teaching of "compensation," being the seed, the precursor to receiving the "wisdom, the teaching of Karma and Reincarnation:"[6]

> Blessed be ye poor; for yours is the kingdom of God. Blessed are ye that hunger now; for ye shall be filled. Blessed are ye that weep now; for ye shall laugh. Blessed are ye when men shall hate you, and when they shall separate you from their company, and shall reproach you, and cast out your name as evil, for the Son of Man's sake. Rejoice ye in that day and leap for joy; for behold your reward is great in heaven [the spiritual worlds].

No matter what your feelings or position on reincarnation may be, it is a concept that is worth understanding more deeply. When we appreciate reincarnation from an evolutionary perspective, it becomes clear that it affords us unique opportunities as we incorporate veil work into our spiritual practice. Reincarnation is a valuable concept to connect to for several reasons:

- It allows the opportunity for compensation—to make amends for wrongs we did to others. Through reincarnation we have the opportunity to redeem our past deeds.
- It allows for human beings and the spiritual beings who dwell in the spiritual world to develop and evolve.

- It offers human beings the opportunity to plant new seeds for our own growth—for example, learning a new skill or exploring a new art form that we can further nurture and develop in our future incarnations.
- It provides the opportunity to take what we have learned in the physical world, meet with higher spiritual beings to review that knowledge, and receive their instruction and guidance for the next incarnation.
- It enables us to become aware of the fact that there are certain things we can only learn and experience on Earth, and that other than the spiritual being the Christ, human beings are the only spiritual beings who are able to come to Earth to learn. The other spiritual beings who make their home solely in the spiritual world do not have that opportunity, so they must learn *through us*.
- It allows us to see the importance of acts of Goodness as seeds for the future. This inspires us to do good works for our loved ones who have died, helping them on their soul's journey in the soul and spiritual worlds and in preparation for their next incarnation.

Influential People Believe in Reincarnation

Many well-known people in a variety of fields have believed in reincarnation and have considered it a spiritual rudder guiding their lives. Henry Ford said, "Genius is experience. Some seem to think that it is a gift or talent, but it is the fruit of long experience in many lives. Some are older souls than others, and so they know more."[7] Carl G. Jung expressed the idea that his life often seemed to be "a story that has no beginning and no end ... I might have lived in former centuries and there encountered questions I was not yet able to answer: that I had been born again because I had not fulfilled the task given to me."[8]

Pythagoras, a Greek philosopher and mathematician, taught that the soul is immortal, resting and being purified in the Underworld between deaths and rebirths; after it has completed this series of rebirths, it becomes so purified that it can leave the transmigration or reincarnation cycle.[9] The author Norman Mailer called himself "a great believer in the hereafter, in karma, in reincarnation. It does make sense. I believe that God is not just a law-giver, but a creative artist.... And what characterizes artists is that they want to redo their work.... Reincarnation is a way for God to improve his earlier works."[10]

According to the Nobel Peace Prize laureate Albert Schweitzer, reincarnation provided "a most comforting explanation of reality by means of which Indian thought surmounts difficulties which baffle the thinkers of Europe."[11] General George S. Patton not only believed in reincarnation but openly spoke about it: "I don't know about other people, but for myself there has never been any question. I don't just think it; I know there are places I've been before, and not in this life."[12]

The great British poet William Wordsworth included these lines in his Immortality Ode:

Our birth is but a sleep and a forgetting:
The Soul that rises with us, our life's star,
Hath had elsewhere its setting,
And cometh from afar ...[13]

Finally, consider Benjamin Franklin, who at the age of twenty-two composed his own mock epitaph:

The Body of B. Franklin,
Printer;
Like the Cover of an old Book,
Its Contents torn out,
And stript of its Lettering and Gilding,

Lies here, Food for Worms.
But the Work shall not be wholly lost.
For it will, as he believ'd, appear once more,
In a new & more perfect Edition,
Corrected and Amended
By the Author.[14]

Breathing Through the Veil

As I continue to experience wonders at the veil, I perceive rein-carnation as a beautiful ebb and flow. We die out of the physical world and are born into the spiritual world. We then die out of the spiritual world and are born into the physical world. It is a breathing back and forth through the veil, with our incarnation into each world being like an inhalation—or inspiration—and our death from it being an exhalation, or expiration. We want to evolve to where we feel that this flow of life and death is truly as natural as breathing. With this knowing comes a letting go of the fear of death.

Consider, too, that our entry from our mother's womb into the world begins with an inhale, and that the last thing we do in the world is to exhale. In this way, our breath at the beginning and ending of physical life offers a kind of mirror image of our movement through the veil.

Breath, Conscious Awareness, and the Still Point

Taking the metaphor a step further, the breath is one of the func-tions of the human body that can take place without our giving it a second thought; we can, and usually do, breathe unconsciously. Similarly, the journeying to and from the spiritual world takes

> *We die out of the physical world and are born
> into the spiritual world. We then die out of
> the spiritual world and are born into
> the physical world. It is a breathing
> back and forth through the veil.*

place whether we are aware of it or not. Many cycles of physical life mirror this breathing process: night at one end of the cycle and day at the other; the seasons of the year—the darkness of winter contrasted with the intense light of summer.

When we bring consciousness to our breathing, we can become aware of the still point: the magical point of rest between when we let go of the breath on an exhale and have to inhale again. The still points in all such natural cycles are subtle doors to the spiritual world, and this is why, as you will discover, the moments of waking and falling asleep provide insight and are especially valuable to us in veil work. All of these "in between" times are openings for us to awaken to, potent times for veil work, and opportunities to feel more alive.

In chapter 1 I mentioned that I am a eurythmist, a practitioner of the form of spiritual movement that Rudolf Steiner developed. In eurythmy we have an effective exercise for working with this image of breathing: we call it Expansion and Contraction. We expand out into the spiritual world and then experience a still point where we have to inwardly determine the point of returning to the Earth in a movement of contraction. This opens our chest area, the heart center. In the Veil Work Activities that follow I will describe this exercise so you can experience it for yourself.

We have a choice: We can go through our lives completely unaware of the breathing back and forth of souls between the physical and spiritual worlds. Or we can choose to consciously investigate, understand, and experience this rhythmic flow through the intentional spiritual practices that are offered in this book. I invite you to choose intentional awareness.

Veil Work Activities

Contemplations

Reincarnation

How do you feel about reincarnation? Does it seem reasonable to you that you are evolving spiritually and that cycles of lifetimes, both in the physical and spiritual worlds, serve the process of your spiritual evolution? When you think about reincarnating after your death, how does it sound? Does returning again and again seem exhausting? Does it feel liberating? Write down your thoughts about reincarnation.

The Cycles of Breathing

Practice noticing the magical moments at the still points in the cycles of life.

Your breathing
Waking and falling asleep
Dawn and dusk
The changing of the seasons

Eurythmy Exercise: Expansion and Contraction

If you are able, stand with your feet on the ground. (If you are unable to stand, you can still experience this exercise sitting upright on a chair).

Bring yourself to a still point with your hands softly crossed at your chest, your heart center, palms open toward your chest, one hand atop the other. Open your arms; start the movement by using the muscles that are closest to the center of your body—your chest muscles in front, scapula area in back—rather than using your hands and arms. Now experiment with opening your arms by leading with your hands. Can you feel the difference? Try it a couple of times if you need to. You should be able to feel that when you start the movement from the center of your chest, your heart center feels more open and expansive.

Even though you start the movement from your center chest area, you still take the movement all the way into the tips of your fingers. As you continue opening your arms, feel yourself expanding/exhaling/excarnating out to the heavens. At a certain point—the still point—you will know it is time to start contracting/inhaling/incarnating back to the physical world. You will feel the heaviness of being pulled through gravity back to Earth. As you contract inward, slowly bring your arms in, still keeping the focus of the movement in your chest/heart area but at the same time continuing to feel down to your fingertips. Bring your hands back to a soft crossed position at your chest. Try this three times.

How did it feel to expand out to the heavens and come back to Earth? Can you feel yourself anew on every cycle of expansion and contraction? What was happening in the moments of still point? How did you know to come to the still point and then move in the other direction?

Further Reading

Here are several well-known titles on the subject of reincarnation. Pick one that sounds juicy, and dive in!

The Soul's Long Journey: How the Bible Reveals Reincarnation by Edward Reaugh Smith, Steiner Books, 2003.

Reincarnation in Christianity: A New Vision of the Role of Rebirth in Christian Thought by Geddes MacGregor, Quest Books, 1990.

Children Who Remember Previous Lives: A Question of Reincarnation by Ian Stevenson, M.D., McFarland & Company, Inc., 2001.

Reincarnation: The Phoenix Fire Mystery, compiled and edited by Sylvia Cranston with a foreword by Elisabeth Kübler-Ross, M.D., Theosophical University Press, 1998.

Reincarnation: A New Horizon in Science, Religion, and Society by Sylvia Cranston and Carey Williams, Julian Press, a division of Crown Publishers, Inc., 1984.

Reincarnation and Karma: Their Significance in Modern Culture by Rudolf Steiner, Anthroposophic Press, 2001.

Ghosts, Spirits & the Afterlife in Native American Folklore and Religion by Gary R. Varner, lulu.com, 2010.

Life After Life by Raymond A. Moody, Jr., M.D., Bantam Books, 1976.

Part 2

Preparation

The next part of this book is about starting your veil work practice on a solid footing. The first step is to get as clear as you can on your intention for the practice—what you want to accomplish and how you plan to approach it, the subject of chapter 3, Defining Your Intention. Chapter 4, Creating Your Journal, will guide you in creating a special "book" that contains tools to help you and your loved one connect. It will also serve as a central place where you can note your experiences. You will be very glad you took this step, especially when you have been doing veil work for a little while, because it will be easy to go back and review significant events and milestones on the exciting journey you are about to undertake. Chapter 5, Setting Up a Successful Practice, is about establishing some structure: essentially, finding ways to make room in your busy life for a dedicated veil work practice.

3

Defining Your Intention

ow it is time to think about why you want to create a veil work practice—what you hope to accomplish and how you want to approach the work—and put it in writing. In this chapter I will suggest some intentions you might consider when you are getting started, but the most important thing is that you settle on one that is meaningful for you, that it is doable in your mind's eye, and that is very clear.

When I started this work years ago, I didn't have a formal written intention. I was moved to do the practice because I knew I wanted to be of service to my daughter. I also wanted to have an understanding of what was going on with her in the spiritual world, so studying Rudolf Steiner's teachings to develop a picture of that was a piece of the puzzle. But I didn't consciously intend to lift the veil between my loved ones and me—that came about as the result of my practice.

Today my intention is clear; I will share it with you a little further on. I now understand how truly helpful it is to have that degree of clarity. That is why I want to support you in creating an intention for your work right from the start, with the understanding that it will most likely change as your practice of veil work deepens and you gain experience.

The Spiritual Force of Intention

> Intent is a force that exists in the universe. When sorcerers beckon intent, it comes to them and sets up the path for attainment, which means that sorcerers always accomplish what they set out to do.
> —Carlos Castaneda[1]

For me, this quote from Carlos Castaneda perfectly describes the importance of intention in guiding the spiritual practice of veil work. I found the quote in Dr. Wayne Dyer's classic book *The Power of Intention*.[2] To clarify, Dyer defines "sorcerers" as "those who live of the Source," which I would further interpret as those who are in connection with the Divine or God. These words give us a powerful image of intention: one beckons the force of intention and it is the *force itself* that actually creates the pathway by which you will reach what you intend.

In his book Dyer identifies four steps for activating your intention. Here's my interpretation of his steps in terms of how they might be helpful in creating a veil work practice.

Discipline
We discipline the physical body so that it may serve our intention. Ideally, in veil work this means getting proper sleep, developing good nutritional habits, avoiding alcohol and drugs, and taking long walks in nature.

*One beckons the force of intention and it is
the force itself that actually creates the pathway
by which you will reach what you intend.*

Wisdom

Dryer writes, "Wisdom combined with discipline fosters your ability to focus and be patient as you harmonize your thoughts, your intellect, and your feelings with the work of your body."[3] I see wisdom in veil work as our ability to cultivate the skill set that it takes to do the practice. This includes understanding the language of the dead and the components of a successful reading practice: our fundamental practice. It means being able to identify signs of co-creation between the living and the dead. And of course it also includes the actual wisdom we gain through studying and reading spiritual materials with our loved ones.

Love

This quality applied to veil work simply asks you to love to do it. When you are clear on your intention and serve from your heart, loving veil work becomes easy.

Surrender

Ah, surrender. This one is not always so easy. Dyer writes that surrender is the "place of intention. This is where your body and your mind aren't running the show and you move into intent."[4] To surrender in veil work, we need to let go of what we think the results should look like.

Your Overall Intention for Veil Work

Until you have been doing veil work for a while and your practice
starts to take a shape that is unique to you, you may find it easiest
to create a single intention that applies to your practice in general.
The first sentence of my own intention that follows is an example of
this. Then, to tailor your intention to the way you plan to practice,
you can add a sentence describing how you plan to fulfill it and
what you are willing to do. Finally, you can ask for assistance.

Essentially, I have turned my intention into a prayer to God:

Dear God,
[Beginning with my intention:] If it is spiritually appropriate, I intend to consciously lift the veil between Lara
and me. [Adding how I am going to do it:] I intend to do
this through continually building my skills as a spiritual
researcher and being of service to Lara by offering her
spiritual nourishment. This will include reading spiritual
materials, practicing eurythmy, and/or doing color work on
a regular basis. [What I am willing to do:] I am open and
receptive to collaborative activities that support Lara in
her current and future spiritual tasks (e.g., learning about
the Word and spiritual aspects of music). [My personal
request/prayer:] Please let me hear what books to read and
how best to be of service. I ask that our guardian angels
be actively engaged in this process and that the Christ
be present throughout our work together. I offer this as a
free deed, with no expectations, while staying open to the
miraculous. Thanks, God. Amen.

Love, Lynn

*Angels are always ready and even eager
to reach across the veil to assist us.*

Note that I added the condition "if it is spiritually appropriate."
Even though I have received the spiritual impulse to fully lift the
veil between myself and my loved ones in the spiritual world, I did
not hear it as a message specific to my relationship with Lara. At
all times throughout this work, I want to know that Lara's spiritual
boundaries are protected and that she remains free. Another form
of this condition is "God's will shall be done."

Also note that I ask our guardian angels for assistance. We will
take a closer look at angels in chapter 5. For now, let me just say
that Rudolf Steiner's work and other sources have taught me that
angels are always ready and even eager to reach across the veil
to assist us. Doing so is their "raison d'être" or "life's work," so to
speak. It is vitally important work in fostering spiritual evolution,
so please do not hesitate to call on them.

Using Your Intention

At the end of this chapter in the activity section, I will take you
through an exercise to help you define your intention. Once you
have decided on it, I recommend that you write it in the dedicated
journal that you will create in the next chapter. You can also write
your intention on a 3 x 5 index card and use it as a bookmark for
the book you are currently reading to your loved one. That way,
each time you sit down to practice veil work, you will be reminded
of the main reason you are doing it—and your loved one will
experience the energy of that intention as well.

Suggested Intentions

Following is a list of ideas to get you started. You are welcome to choose one of these during this chapter's exercise or to develop something else from your own vision of your desired outcome.

- To provide spiritual nourishment for your loved one
- To consciously deepen your love for them
- To heal a past wound
- To provide guidance for your loved one as they journey through the spiritual worlds
- To co-create with your loved one activities that support their spiritual growth—and yours
- To provide spiritual information for a task that your loved one may want to complete in his or her next incarnation
- To assist yourself in completing a spiritual task
- To connect more deeply with your loved one and develop your relationship in a new and inspiring way
- To serve God's plan for human spiritual evolution
- To increase your own spiritual capacities by learning to see and hear the language of those in the spiritual world
- To be inspired to explore new areas of spiritual study and activities that are new to you

This last point suggests that as your work develops and grows, your loved one might inspire you to learn the spiritual aspects of common human activities. You might delve into the spiritual nature of the arts, including music, speech, and writing. Or you might be moved to explore other aspects of "regular" life that really need to be spiritualized: agriculture, business, community life, or the study of the stars. We will talk more about a whole range of activities when we discuss reading to your loved ones. For now, just remember that when these new spiritual impulses come to you, you might find it helpful to write a new intention that supports you in achieving an

---

*Get in the habit of writing down your intention—
it will help you remember to bring your loved ones
into your work.*

---

appropriate outcome in that area.

Today when I am actively engaged in a spiritual activity, my intention for it comes fairly easily. Before I dive in, I consciously set an intention to bring that activity to Lara and the others I am in touch with across the veil. If I am working on a project that I feel is inspired by my loved ones, one that I want them to be involved in, or one where I could use their assistance, I create an intention tailored to that. Recent examples in my life include writing this book, doing eurythmy sessions with an intentional community for people with disabilities, and completing a color exercise designed to help me meet my loved ones at the threshold.

Depending on the duration of the project or activity, I may or may not write the intention down. For writing this book—a big project—I wrote a specific intention. When I am teaching a eurythmy session, however, I don't write anything down. Instead, I intentionally bring my loved ones into the activity in my mind and heart, in the moment. You will know what is appropriate for you as your own practice unfolds. At the beginning, though, I suggest you get in the habit of writing down your intention—it will help you remember to bring your loved ones into your work.

Intentions for Specific Activities

Reading
For me, reading spiritual materials is the foundation of my practice, and that is why I have presented it in this book as the most essential

practice. It is the work that anchors my connection to my daughter and others. At times when I feel disconnected, I know that if I intensify my efforts to read to my loved ones, I will regain the connection immediately. That means investing more time (for example, expanding my reading time from thirty minutes to an hour or more) and reading in an environment that best supports me in bringing my attention into focus. Some days that might mean sitting at the kitchen table and other days sitting more relaxed on the couch.

Your intention for reading can be as simple as the first one on my list of suggestions: providing spiritual nourishment. You might add the intention to have complete faith that your loved ones are receiving the spiritual content in the material you are reading. Or your reading intention can be focused on choosing the appropriate material to read, something you will learn more about in part 4.

As you continue your reading practice, you might receive an impulse to focus on a particular area of study. One that has come up for me is the study of the Word (explored in greater depth in chapter 16 on eurythmy) and the creative forces that stand behind the sounds of words. While it has been lost to most of modern society, previous cultures recognized and revered the power contained within spoken sounds and knew that they were the building blocks to creating what words represent. This study is directly related to Lara and my other loved ones across the veil, because their home is where the creative forces are found. For that reason, I thought it merited a more specific intention:

> My intention is to convey to Lara a conscious understanding of the creative forces that stand behind the sounds of words. I will research and study experts in the area of the Word. Some of the resources I will tap into are my eurythmy sources, the Bible (in particular Genesis and Saint John's Gospel) and the work of Rudolf Steiner, Kenneth Copeland, and Robert Tennyson Stevens. I will stay open to God's

will and inspiration from my loved ones, and I ask for a full understanding of what I am reading.

Color

As I have indicated, color is another way to offer spiritual nourishment to those who have died. That in itself can be your sole intention for a session during which you work or play with color—and that intention is plenty! But you may also set the intention to understand the spiritual quality of a particular color. I will give you more information on the spiritual nature of color in chapter 15, but to offer an example, cobalt blue carries the spiritual essence of devotion. Your intention might be *to expand my soul experience of cobalt blue through exploring and journaling what devotion means*. To do that, you might answer a couple of questions: Are there particular spiritual leaders whom you admire because of their devotional nature? What behaviors do they exhibit that exemplify devotion? Then when you paint or color with cobalt blue, you can notice how your soul experience of that color has changed and capture those observations in your journal.

Other Areas

Here are a few other subject-specific intentions:

Music: *My intention is to investigate and study the spiritual nature of tones and intervals.*

Astronomy: *My intention is to investigate and study the spiritual nature of stars.*

Spiritual leadership: *My intention is to investigate and study the spiritual thread through all faiths and the qualities of spiritual leaders of all faiths.*

Business: *My intention is to investigate and study how to spiritualize business practices.*

To any intention about something you are learning you can add "I ask that my loved one learn alongside me and fully participate in this quest."

Community: *My intention is to investigate and study how individuals, reflecting spiritual truths through their behavior, can enhance community life.*

To add a request to any of these intentions, you can include a sentence like this: *I ask that my loved one learn alongside me and fully participate in this quest.*

Veil Work Activity: Define Your Intention

Hopefully this discussion has given you some good ideas for where to start in defining your intention and how to bring some clarity to what you are willing to do to realize it. Now it's your turn.

First, create a quiet space for yourself. Have paper available and a pen that you would like to dedicate to this work. If you enjoy the ritual of lighting a candle, please do that.

Now envision your loved one and your guiding angels or other spiritual beings you would like to have present with you. Speak aloud into the space a favorite prayer, poem, or verse from a poem. Take a moment to be still in your mind, and be open to images of what working together with your loved one might look like. Try not to censor these; allow yourself to receive the images without judging them and write them down as fast as you can; like dreams, images from the spiritual world sometimes dissipate quickly. Then, once you have captured a list of the images you received, choose the image that you most resonate with or that you feel is most doable. Keep the entire list of images, along with your loved one's name, and be sure to date it. It will be both fun and illuminating to revisit this list in three or four months.

If you weren't able to come up with any images, not to worry—developing the sensitivity to receive can take time. Instead you can write down thoughts or feelings about what you would like to see happen as an outcome of your service to your loved one.

If you are still coming up empty, go back to the list I offered on page 42 and write down two or three intentions that resonate with you. Trust that your intention will become more refined as you continue reading and working on the activities in this book.

Now write down at least three ideas for your intention and finish the sentences for each one.

1. An idea I have for my intention is:
   How I am going to do this:
   What I am willing to do:
   My personal request/prayer:

2. An idea I have for my intention is:
   How I am going to do this:
   What I am willing to do:
   My personal request/prayer:

3. An idea I have for my intention is:
   How I am going to do this:
   What I am willing to do:
   My personal request/prayer:

From this list, choose one and write it again as a complete statement:

My intention and prayer for my spiritual practice with [insert your loved one's name] is:

To complete the creation of your intention, speak it aloud to your loved one and your angels or other spiritual beings you would like to help you. Send the image of your intention to your loved one, and see them receiving it.

Take a moment of gratitude for your spiritual practice. Blow out your candle. Put your writings in a safe place so you may draw upon them for the journal that you will be making next, in chapter 4.

4

Creating Your Journal

You have settled on an intention for your veil work practice, and you have put that down on paper. Now it's time to set up a journal dedicated solely to this work and record your intention there. Creating your journal will help you focus, ground your practice, and track your experiences.

This first journal may look different from your future journals in that it is really part journal and part companion workbook for this book. Each chapter of this book includes activities to help you anchor the techniques and skills you will be learning. You will log these exercises in your journal, documenting your experiences and using them to guide your future practice. You may come back to this book as a reference as well, and I hope you do, but my aim is for your journal to become your unique guide to the techniques and tools *you* have used to cultivate your practice.

When I first started to do veil work, I never thought that my life would be so affected by my relationships with those in the spiritual world. Through the years since, I have made random notes in numerous personal journals, occasionally jotting down what spiritual materials I read and the date, and I have made random notations and date entries in the books and lectures I have read pertaining

---

*Your journal will help you shape a practice
that fits your personal lifestyle and spiritual path.*

---

to this spiritual practice. However, it did not occur to me until relatively recently to start a journal specific to veil work, not only to capture my own personal narrative of this intimate experience, but to serve as a reference for research and to offer a template for others to use. Now that I have created a journal—based on the insights I have gained in more than eighteen years of practice—I can't emphasize enough the value of this down-to-earth tool, and I know it will greatly benefit you if you start yours now. If I'd had such a journal when I first started reading to Lara, I would have been able to start from a stronger and more supported base, and I would now have a record of those early, eye-opening days as my communication with Lara, my parents, and others began to unfold and develop. But I was finding my way then, picking up my cues from Rudolf Steiner's writings and exploring on my own. I had not yet learned what a wonderful touchstone, companion, and research document a journal can be. Fortunately, you can have your journal ready to go on day one!

The Value of a Journal

Your journal will help you shape a practice that fits your personal lifestyle and spiritual path by helping you set up your own system for working with your loved ones. The entries I suggest putting in your journal will also serve you in many other ways. Your journal will:

- Reinforce your intention for your work.

- Support you in choosing which books to read to your loved ones.
- Help you identify who is trying to connect with you, especially when your practice includes developing relationships with several loved ones.
- Assist you in identifying the co-creative opportunities your loved ones are presenting to you.
- Be a tool to ignite your imagination with sensory memories of your loved ones, reminding you of what they were like when they were alive and bringing the experience of them closer to you. This will deepen your connection and make it easier for you and your loved ones to "find" each other.
- Be a great place to record your own personal research. You will be surprised at the random moments of inspiration that arise—feelings, thoughts, and questions—as a result of your practice. You will want to note these inspirations as well as any patterns you observe.
- Hold copies of any photographs and handwriting samples you may have that evoke your loved ones' specific character qualities.
- Personalize the entire experience, honoring the unique relationship you and your loved ones now share.
- Form a living document of your work and experiences in real time as they unfold.
- Serve as an enduring, sacred record of your commitment to your loved ones and of all the gifts and surprises you encounter in your service to and potential collaboration with them.
- Serve as a research document others can learn from if you choose to share your results and findings.

What This Journal Is Not

I do not recommend that you use this journal to process all the many feelings and thoughts you have about your loved one and their death—at least not pages and pages of processing. It can be very valuable to write it all out, however. So if you find it helpful to write pages and pages, go ahead and give yourself free rein using a separate journal. Dedicate this one solely to the spiritual practice of veil work.

Focus on One Person at First

For the remainder of this chapter, let us assume that you will focus on one person at a time in your journal, beginning with your "primary" loved one, the person who most inspired you to begin veil work practice. All the steps you take for this person you can take for others when you become more familiar with the practice.

Choose Your Own Journaling Style

Also, I would like to suggest that if you are not up to or interested in creating an extensive, "artistic" journal such as I describe here, you can adapt these ideas to work for your personality and style. Know that writing your observations and answers in a simple blank book or notebook using an ordinary pen or pencil will be fine.

Prepare to Create Your Journal— Gather Photos and Handwriting Samples

Before you sit down to actually construct your journal, you will want to gather these important elements.

In his book *Staying Connected*, Rudolf Steiner writes, "By concentrating on handwriting or a picture, we take into our own work the dead person's views, intentions, and aims."[1] I suggest you choose a photo that best exemplifies who your loved one was as a person. For the handwriting sample, the writing itself does not have to be particularly meaningful: a grocery list jotted on a slip of paper or an address on an envelope will work perfectly well. Or you can use a cherished handwritten note.

Before we go any further, I would like to mention two important considerations. First, I recommend using *copies* of photos and handwriting samples, not originals. You want to be at ease when you're leafing through your journal, not worried that you will damage something that's irreplaceable. Second, if you don't have a photo or handwriting sample, that is fine. They are wonderful to have but not essential for this work. The following section called "Meaningful Memories" gives you a range of other ways to connect with your loved one.

To give you examples of the kinds of photos and handwriting samples you could select, I will share with you what materials I gathered for Lara and my mother. For Lara's journal section, I chose a family photo of her and me, made a copy that was a tad larger than the original photo, and then cut the background away. I love this photo. Lara's smile is beaming, expressing the delight she felt after swimming with her father beneath a small waterfall while we were vacationing in eastern Pennsylvania.

On my first journal page dedicated to memories of my mother, I placed my favorite photo of her—smiling at Dad behind the camera while they were at the beach in sunny Southern California. For a handwriting sample, I found in one of my mother's old recipe books a recipe she had jotted down called "Two Minute Cake," which I photocopied and placed in my journal. When I look at this little sample of her handwriting, I can immediately picture my mother standing at her kitchen counter and "feel into" the person she was.

*Identifying a personality gesture
your loved one had is something else
you can do to retrieve a sensory memory.*

Meaningful Memories

Here are some other ways to deepen your connection to your loved one, any of which you can include in your journal. Some of them can also prompt ideas for your book reading practice and may be helpful to you in identifying co-creative projects for you and your loved one. You can choose to work with all of these ideas or just one or two.

Sensory Images of Your Loved One

If you were physically close to your loved one, recall what it felt like to touch them. Write down a few words about that. I have re-created the image and feeling of Lara sitting pressed against my chest thousands and thousands of times, so I do not need a photo to remind me. And you might feel the same about your loved one—that you do not need anything more than your memory to bring them close.

Another way I have gathered sensory images is by actively embodying the person's physical nature. Because Lara had physical disabilities, after she died I spent time lying on the floor trying to sense what it might feel like to have been in her body—a body that often could not do what she wanted it to do.

You can also access a memory of a specific physical aspect of your loved one. A physical memory of my mother involves the piano. Growing up I had many occasions to watch my mother play. I remember always being attracted to and fascinated by the way her hands moved across the keys. Now I am taking lessons, and sometimes when I practice I see my mother's hands—even though mine are shaped entirely different from hers. As my fingers search for the correct keys to strike, I feel my hands as slender and graceful, like hers.

Identifying a personality gesture your loved one had is something else you can do to retrieve a sensory memory. An example of this for me immediately brings me an inner chuckle. My dad had a very mischievous side. And accompanying this mischievousness came a smile and a certain look on his face, one that I often recognize in both of my brothers. So if you are having a hard time thinking of a gesture, look at some of your family members who are still living because we can often find these personality gestures passed down.

Jot down any thoughts or feelings that come up as you recall these kinds of physical senses or gestures.

Notable Things Your Loved One Said, to You or Someone Else

Did this person say something to you when they were alive that made you feel especially close to them? Did they say something that changed your life in some way? Did they say something that made you laugh until tears streamed down your face? Has someone else told you about something memorable your loved one said? Capture those words in your journal.

I remember having a conversation with my mother a few weeks before she died. I had told her that I was trying to get pregnant, and she was thrilled. She looked straight into my eyes and told me how pleased she was, and that I had so much love to give. After Lara was born and I was a somewhat insecure new mother, my mother's words rose in my memory, soothed my insecurities, and gave me courage. Now, twenty-eight years later, I can still re-create the memory in mind. We were in her bedroom. My mother was sitting in a chair by the window and I was sitting very close to her, right

---

How would you describe who this person was as an individual? What were their qualities?

---

at her feet. The memory of those words and that moment still fills my heart with great warmth and invites me to sense my mother's presence—even now as I write about this experience.

The Essence of Your Loved One

How would you describe who this person was as an individual? What were their qualities? Were they warm? Thoughtful? Bossy? Fun loving? Studious? Easygoing? Ambitious? Write down a few key qualities you observed when they were alive, words that describe their essential self.

For example, Lara had a huge capacity for what I would call "generous love." I saw it in her as she watched another child move her body with so much ease, something she could not do. Her facial expression radiated, "Oh, look how beautifully she is moving her body!"

My mother's essence included a keen ability to discern a person's character as well as a love of the virtue of Beauty. I made sure to note those diverse qualities in my journal.

Your Loved One's Contribution to the World

What gifts did this person offer to the world? These could be actual physical contributions, intangible ones, or both. Did they offer mentorship? Music? Wit? A fantastic recipe? A clever invention? A healing massage? Courage? Integrity? Wisdom? Write down these contributions.

Lara made a significant impression on her fellow students, parents, and teachers while she attended kindergarten. She was the first child with disabilities to go to this particular public school.

While she was fully embraced by most people, there were some who—I can only guess out of ignorance—were uncomfortable with Lara being fully included in the "regular" classroom. These few, parents mainly, felt that my daughter should attend a classroom designated for children with disabilities, and thought that Lara would somehow take away from their children's experience and learning. Yet the incredible support of Lara's speech therapist, conversations with teachers and parents, and the experience of the children in her classroom all revealed that Lara's presence was actually a gift to the children and their learning experience. It shifted people's social consciousness and inspired a new way for the school to welcome other children with disabilities. Lara, too, received gifts—the gifts of love and educational support.

Noting in your journal the positive impacts your loved one had on others while they were living is a wonderful way for you to connect with them.

Incompletions

Did your loved one feel that they were unable to complete something during their life? Was something left undone? Did they hold any regrets? Did they have a special skill set or talent that they were not able to fully develop?

With this one, I often think of my mother. She never told me directly, but I always perceived her as feeling incomplete when it came to expressing and cultivating her native talents as an artist and designer. If you know of a longing your loved one had that was not fulfilled during their life, noting that in your journal can be very fruitful, especially when you begin thinking about the spiritual materials you would like to read to them and the co-creative activities the two of you can engage in together.

A Favorite Prayer, Poem, Song, or Book

Remember: all of the elements you add to your journal provide a means of connection to your loved one and offer ways to be of

---

Appreciation is a wonderful way to strengthen connection. What are you most grateful to your loved one for?

---

service to them, including discerning which books to read to them and which projects to co-create. As you will learn in chapter 9 when you explore the reading practice, you will begin by reading a prayer, a poem, a verse from a poem, or even song lyrics. Sometimes using a passage that was your loved one's favorite, or that they found particularly meaningful when they were living, adds powerfully to your practice. If you write these short pieces down in your journal, you will have a handy reference for later, and if they had a favorite spiritual book, you can note that as well.

What They Did That You Are Grateful For

Appreciation is a wonderful way to strengthen connection. What are you most grateful to your loved one for? Is your life different today because your loved one was in it? Did this person invite you to a party—the same party where you met your future spouse? Did they encourage you to complete your college education, perhaps even by paying your tuition costs?

Did your loved one do something as dramatic as saving your life? When I was about seven years old, I was sucking on a sourball candy and it got lodged in my throat. Fortunately, my dad was nearby. Moving quickly, he grabbed me and literally turned me upside down and thumped me on the back—out came the sourball. Until I did this work I really didn't think, *Oh! My dad actually saved my life that day!* This incident definitely goes on my dad's memory page as a big gratitude.

As you can see, there are many ways you can evoke your loved one to make it easier for the two of you to connect, and all of these can find a home in your journal.

Now it is time to put that journal together.

Create Your Journal

Gather Your Art Supplies
The materials you select to create your journal are highly individual and can be as simple or as elaborate as you like. Here is a short list of items:

The journal itself. In working with a variety of journals and note-books over the years, I have discovered one that I think is perfect for this initial journal, and I invite you to try it. It is a nine-by-twelve-inch spiral-bound sketchbook with sixty-pound paper. A good one to look for is the Strathmore 400 Field Sketchbook, which contains seventy sheets of acid-free recycled sketch paper. The spiral binding is handy because the journal lies flat, and the sixty-pound paper is heavy enough to stand up to the watercolor exercises we will do in chapters 6 and 15.

An assortment of colored markers, colored pens, colored pencils, watercolors, pastels, and crayons. These are for your own choosing and artistic preferences and you will use them mainly for decorating your journal pages. For the activity exercises in the chapters, I will also make specific suggestions for any additional art supplies you may need.

Glue sticks for affixing photos, handwriting samples, or other items onto the pages.

Other embellishments including construction paper or other colored or patterned papers, glitter, stickers, rubber stamps, or stencils. Items found in nature are another option: dried flowers or leaves, for example—anything that can be pasted in place.

Assemble Your Journal

You will want to set aside forty-five minutes to two hours just to be with the process of creating your journal. You do not have to do this all in one session. I invite you to take your time, play with it, and let your intuition be your guide as you follow the template I offer in the next section. This journal will be unique to you and your loved one, and it will reflect your unique connection. Everything you place on its pages will let your loved one shine through.

However, here are some thoughts to have in mind as you begin. Do be sure that your environment is calm and somewhat orderly. Creating your journal is actually one of the first stages of making your intention known to your loved one that *YES! I want to build a conscious relationship with you!* So attending to the environment is important.

Veil Work Practice: Use This Template to Create Your Journal

The following is a sample template for setting up a seventy-page journal.

> *Cover page.* Decorate this page in a way that is meaningful for you. Your artwork might embody a theme that connects you to your loved one. Theme ideas include: nature, colors of the rainbow, the stars, a song, or even a fairy tale. You might even explore creating a title for your journal, like a book title, describing the relationship you have with your primary loved one.

First page—your intention for the work. Revisit the intention you created in chapter 3 and sit with it again for a few moments. Try it on for size. Does it still resonate? If it does, you're all set. If you're not 100 percent sure, you're still all set because your intention can evolve over time, just as the exact ways you will wind up serving your loved one are not set in stone. As your communication with them unfolds, you may gain clarity you don't yet have, or your practice may lead you to expand your intention or see it somewhat differently. If, now that you are reviewing it, you know there's something about your intention that you want to change, that's fine—go right ahead. Otherwise, if it seems like you're at least on the right track, capture that intention on this page using the writing implement of your choice, and date it.

Your Loved One's Page. This page is dedicated to your primary loved one. Here is what I recommend placing on this page:

The person's full name given at birth and any nicknames

Their date of birth and their death date

A photo and/or handwriting sample

Answers to any of the topics in the above section titled "Meaningful Memories"

Artistic tip: You can decorate each page as you desire, using the art supplies you have gathered. Once you begin your practice, however, I do recommend consistently putting the date on every entry—you will be glad you did. You can write it very small.

Reserve the remaining pages of your journal for chapter notes, exercises, and activities. You might want to divide the pages according to the chapters in this book, allowing a few pages for each one.

I hope you find creating your journal meaningful and satisfying—and even joyful! Next we will talk about how to establish a successful practice—another building block in your preparation for veil work.

5

Setting Up a Successful Practice

Veil work is by its nature devotional work. It requires a committed, steady practice. This is not always easy for us to achieve in our busy lives. After Lara's death, I was blessed with the time to fully establish a successful rhythm of daily reading, which then led to the co-creative activities with my loved ones you will read about in later chapters.

This is not to say that there haven't been days when I have felt less than successful in my practice of veil work. Unplanned life events will always present themselves, requiring me to consciously choose to maintain my practice day by day.

I actually like that life demands that I continually ask myself, "Do I do this practice of veil work out of my own personal freedom—without taking on guilt if I miss providing some sort of spiritual nourishment to my loved one for a day? Or am I wanting something from it: a spiritual favor, perhaps, or a message from my loved one?" Yes, I enjoy summoning the devotion for this work, yet at the same time I am wise enough to set up structures in my life to support a successful practice. I trust that, like me, you are open to receiving support for a consistent practice, and on that note, I

---

*I suggest you set aside a specific time each day
for a planned session of veil work.*

---

will share some tips that have helped me create a lasting practice that bears fruit for myself and for my loved ones.

A Consistent Rhythm

> We are what we repeatedly do.
> Excellence, then, is not an act, but a habit.
> —Will Durant on Aristotle[1]

This is probably the most important element of a successful practice: a consistent rhythm that develops into a habit. I suggest you set aside a specific time each day for a planned session of veil work. For me, early mornings are best. The quiet hours before the rest of the world awakes are my favorite. The veil is more approachable then, and for me, these hours seem to be the most sacred and spirit filled. This is my dedicated time when I put everything else aside and sit down to do a reading session and my personal eurythmy practice with my loved ones. My other collaborative practices are woven into the day based on my schedule.

You might encounter resistance to these regular practice sessions—from yourself or from others who desire your time. I have found that *declaring* that the morning is my time for my veil work has been helpful. Declarations have tremendous power. Anyone who has read much of the Bible knows the power of the spoken word. In Genesis 1:3–26, while in the process of creating the world, God brings things into existence through His words. You will find in these verses numerous instances of the words "And God said,

'Let ...'" followed by the manifestation response "And it was so." He declared the world into existence, and it "was." That's how powerful His Word is.

Let the power of your spoken word work on your behalf. Find a time of day that is best for you and declare it's your time. If need be, wake up a half hour earlier or let go of something that is less important to you. Given a little time, your regular sessions will become a habit, one that offers comfort, delight, and a world filled with possibilities.

In his book *The 7 Habits of Highly Successful People*, Dr. Steven Covey defines a habit as "the intersection of *knowledge, skill,* and *desire.*" He goes on to say, "Knowledge is the theoretical paradigm, the *what to do* and the why. Skill is the *how to do.* And desire is the motivation, the *want to do.* In order to make something a habit in our lives, we have to have all three."[2]

With this book I hope to give you the knowledge, skill, and desire to establish a personal practice of veil work *as a habit.*

At this point for me, it's hard to imagine going through a day without actively connecting with my loved ones who have died. Cultivating my reading practice into a habit built my capacity to fold veil work into my everyday life. Now it is normal for me to bring my loved ones in at various times of the day. I can do this while driving to an appointment, making dinner, sitting at my piano lesson, or listening to a symphony performance. It is a skill that I cherish and recognize as a grace in my life.

In a way, this rhythm of consistency is an extension of the breathing in and out through the veil itself, the beautiful ebb and flow between Earth and the spiritual world. Your consistent practice of veil work is your own echo of that rhythm, carried through into the physical world.

The rhythm of consistency is an extension of the breathing in and out through the veil itself.

When Consistency Is Not Possible

All that said, there will be times when you are simply not able to show up for your practice at the usual time. You may be traveling and away from your usual veil work "station," the place you have carefully set up to be conducive to your reading sessions and other practices. You may be at home but experiencing some type of upheaval in your life: a distressing kind of disruption like a loved one getting sick and requiring your care, or falling ill yourself. Or it could be a delightful interruption—a big reunion of extended family with people coming and going everywhere, seasonal holiday celebrations, or being totally focused on a rewarding work project that has a specific deadline. This kind of "stuff of life" happens to all of us, and it is all part of the richness of life.

In situations such as these, when I'm not able to practice as I usually do, I like to do a less formal version of the practice any time I think of it during the day. My informal practice is very simple: I bring my loved one into my heart and mind and serve them in one of the following ways through a combination of imagination and the activity itself. I might:

- Do a eurythmy I-A-O (see pages 218 through 221 for instruction on this practice)
- Remember a specific memory of my loved one and infuse that memory with love and gratitude
- Share classical music during my piano practice time

- Share with them in my imagination the colors I see in nature as I drive to an appointment
- Say a prayer

I would like to acknowledge at this point that veil work is a very private thing, and you may not want to practice it in the kinds of circumstances I have outlined, with other people bustling around. Yet I encourage you to give it a try anyway and see what happens. The people you are with when "life happens" do not need to know that you are practicing veil work at all. Remember: a big part of this practice consists of utilizing your imagination, and that is something you can do while waiting for a plane or doing prep chef duties for the family picnic. Remember, too, that the still points I mentioned in chapter 2, those magical times of waking and falling asleep each day, are always available to you and are potent times for veil work practice. Even if you forget to practice at any other time of the day, if you have been consistently doing your practice at those times, you can keep that continuity going no matter what else may be happening in your life.

Faith

In addition to a consistent rhythm, another quality that will be a great help in sustaining your practice is to keep the faith. In fact, there is a useful formula to keep in mind:

Rhythm + Faith = Commitment

The virtue of faith inspires us to believe when there is no proof. In our work, when I speak of cultivating the virtue of faith I am talking about taking it on faith that what you are doing is genuinely

---

If you hang in there during times of doubt,
you will be so glad you kept your practice alive
when you sense the certainty of contact.

---

serving your loved one on their spiritual journey even if you don't receive clear proof that your work has reached them. This is part of the selflessness of the practice: faith means allowing yourself a feeling of confidence that spiritual evolution—yours, your loved one's, and in fact everyone's—is being served through your practice.

Because I have never doubted my spiritual reading reaches Lara or my loved ones, faith is not something that I struggle with. But I appreciate that it could be difficult to maintain a successful practice if you are unsure that your efforts are having any impact. If you do wrestle with it, I can share with you that at this point in my own practice I have had many clear indications that my service is being received and is of value. If you have any doubts, I believe that you, too, will know within a short time that your loved one is receiving your work. The communication channels are open, and loving service is flowing through them all the time—service that can become a cornerstone of your life.

At times, though, you may grow impatient because you are not seeing "signs" that you are getting through—or you are not recognizing signs when they appear. You may even feel like you want to demand some form of evidence as a condition of continuing to do the work. It just does not work that way, and that's why you need to have faith. It is worth it to hang in there during times of doubt. When you do sense the certainty of contact, you will be so glad you kept your practice alive and moved through and past that doubt.

Structuring for Success

A certain amount of self-knowledge can be a huge help in veil work, especially when it comes to understanding your patterns of resistance. We can all point to things we resist despite knowing that they are "good for us," that they are things we "should" do. We all have strategies for avoiding such beneficial activities. It is worth thinking about what your own strategies are for resisting good things or for "falling out of the habit" of doing them. Then come up with ways to lessen your resistance. Here are a few techniques that have worked for me. You might give them a try too.

- Prepare your reading space before you go to bed at night so it is there waiting for you in the morning. Make the space an inviting and special one. Place fresh flowers there. Try an aromatherapy scent. Sometimes I like to use the fragrances of the essential oils people used during biblical times, especially if I plan to read from the Bible. Pay attention to the lighting, and to the colors in this space. The goal is to make it a place where you just want to be, plain and simple, a place where you feel safe and relaxed and ready to explore.

- Journal about your resistance. What thoughts and feelings are attached to it? Can you identify any rationalizations you are making, or unrealistic assumptions? Write down a few lines about why you desired to do this practice in the first place—why you decided it was important to you. Remembering your desire can serve as inspiration. My desires for writing this book, for example—a recent development in my veil work practice—are to illuminate a subject that no one else is writing about and to honor Lara's life. When my "resistance thoughts" arise, this gives them a reminder of why they are not useful.

If you are having difficulty establishing a steady practice, call on your angels to help you.

- Find interest in what you have chosen to do, whether it is the material you plan to read or some other activity you have settled on. This is the antidote to the "shoulds." If you have selected something that truly interests you, your "should" will become "desire to." Are you drawn to playing with color? Is there a book that always seems to leave you with a lighter heart than you had when you sat down to read? Is there a subject matter you can offer to your loved one that *you* find compelling and engaging? If the actual content of what you are offering your loved one is something that inspires you, it will hold your interest and you will want to do your practice session because it makes you feel more alive.

Ask for Help: Your Angels Await Your Call

You are not alone when you work at the veil. As I've said before, your loved ones are eager to help you, but you actually have many more potential allies than that. There are angelic beings in the spiritual world that are waiting for you to call upon them.

If you are not used to calling on your angels—or even thinking about angels at all—it may be helpful to give you some orientation. As Christian Community priest Reverend Cynthia Hindes writes, "We each have an angel assigned to us, a guardian angel, who accompanies us along our paths through lifetimes.... The angel's 'eyes,' angelic consciousness, see, take in, and remember everything for us.... [and] radiate toward us love and recognition of our true being.... They [guardian angels] have devoted their being to ours."

Hindes adds that the spiritual world has given us the gift of freedom, and that while angels "may gently suggest" through inspirations and thoughts, whether and how we respond is for us to decide.[3]

An Angel Speaks

O if you knew how your countenance
is changed, when in the midst
of that pure gaze which can unite you with me
Your hold upon yourself is lost
And you turn away.
Just as a landscape in clear light
May suddenly cloud over, do you close
Yourself against me, and *I have to wait
And wait in silence, often long* [emphasis mine].
And if I were like you a human being
The pain of disdained love would kill me.
But since the Father has given me unending patience
I wait for you unshaken
and expectant, whenever it may be you come.
And even this gentle reproach
Take not as reproach—only as a pure message.[4]

Jeremy Smith, a student of Rudolf Steiner's work, writes:

Each of us—you, me, every one—has a guardian angel. Our very own dedicated guide in the spiritual world, it envelops us in unconditional love. Our angel gives us the safe space in which our higher selves can develop and eventually come into independent maturity. Impulses from our angel allow true ideas to stream into our consciousness. These guide us in our earthly tasks and relationships and give us strength to overcome the inevitable challenges we all meet along the way.

Delving further into the angelic realms, Smith describes archangels as spiritual beings who "unite groups of people, who have a common purpose or mission, by flowing in rhythmic motion amongst group members and their angels." They "give strength to each individual human ... [and] inspire and give courage to each member of the group to work together to fulfill their common tasks." As veil workers, we are a community of people who share the common goal of developing veil work further. Archangels, then, are our willing allies in this endeavor.

Other spiritual beings that can support us in veil work include the archai, who "help us attune our efforts so as to be most fruitful at a particular time and place."[5] Now is the time in human evolution to bring veil work to the broader community, and the archai are here to support us in this.

Veil Work Activities

Creating a Habit

Let's look at Dr. Covey's definition of *habit* again: "the intersection of *knowledge*, *skill*, and *desire*.... Knowledge is the theoretical paradigm, the *what to do* and the *why*. Skill is the *how to do*. And desire is the motivation, the *want to do*. In order to make something a habit in our lives, we have to have all three."

Working with his model, consider the following statements and fill in the blanks:

Knowledge

Assess your knowledge on the subject of veil work practice:

I may or may not know that my loved ones are trying to connect and collaborate with me. I may or may not know that I have the capacity to connect and collaborate with them.

The "what to do" about this is: my veil practice.
Why do I want to do it?

_____

_____

Skill

How to do it. Before you progress further in this book, identify and define three critical skills that you feel might be important to bring to or cultivate in your veil work practice.

1.
2.
3.

Desire

Unless I really desire to do veil work, it won't become a habit in my life.

I want to do veil work because:

_____

_____

Or it's possible that you are just curious about veil work and don't have any intention to develop this as a spiritual practice. Fair enough. If that is the case I invite you to clarify your thoughts further by stating: I do not want to do veil work because:

_____

_____

Or maybe you are not sure about committing full time to a veil work practice. In that case, I invite you to commit to the practice for a set amount of time, say one to three months, and then reevaluate your commitment.

Resistance

Do you feel that you might have some resistance to veil work? If so, take a moment to journal about the resistance you feel and where you envision it might pop up in your own practice.

Declaration

What are you willing to declare regarding making the time to do your veil work practice? Feel free to write your declaration out here and then speak it.

_____

_____

What structures would be helpful for you to have in place as you envision your veil work practice?

_____

_____

Your Guardian Angel, the Archangel, and the Archai Supporting Your Veil Work

What is your current relationship with your guardian angel?

How can you see this angel supporting you?

Can you envision the community of people doing veil work being guided by an archangel? How does it feel to be part of this community?

Can you envision the archai of this work supporting the timing of veil work, supporting the idea that, indeed, *now* is the time?

Further Reading

The 7 Habits of Highly Effective People: Powerful Lessons in Personal Change by Stephen R. Covey, Simon & Schuster, 1989.
Angels by Rudolf Steiner, Rudolf Steiner Press, 1996.

Part 3

Communication Basics

You have accomplished a great deal by this point in the book. You have a good overview of veil work and its role in spiritual evolution, and you have put structures in place to support you in building a strong practice. Now it is time to talk about the reason you have invested this time and energy: connecting with your loved one!

We'll begin this part with a discussion of some of the qualities you want to bring to communication from your side of the veil. Chapter 6, Cultivating a Mood, covers being present and bringing soulful qualities to the work. The next two chapters cover the two sides of the communication equation, with chapter 7, Reaching Through the Veil, being about reaching out to your loved ones, and chapter 8, Receiving Through the Veil, covering the many ways in which you might expect to receive messages from them.

6

Cultivating a Mood

*T*his chapter is short but very important. In the last chapter, I offered suggestions to help you establish a successful practice, including setting up an inviting physical environment. Your mental, emotional, and spiritual environment—the mood you establish—is equally important, so that is what we will discuss in this chapter.

The Gift of Your Presence

The most important factor in cultivating the appropriate mood for your practice is to be *fully present* to the experience.

Most people I know lead very busy lives, and you probably do too. You have work and family commitments. You might have volunteer work. You may have commitments to yourself as well, such as getting regular exercise, or taking time to de-stress after a demanding workday. And then there are relationships with friends and family to nurture, and time to simply enjoy life and have fun.

Not only do we typically pack a lot of different activities into a day, we often do several things at once! We might catch up on the

The moments shared with your loved one
are made more valuable to both of you
when you fully embody the present moment.

news while cooking dinner or plan the day's itinerary in the shower. We often move distractedly through the items on our to-do lists.

Your new spiritual practice is an entirely different experience. Serving your loved one means giving them the gift of your undivided presence. Of course, that starts with your making time to do the practice. But just as important is the *quality of attention* you bring to that dedicated time. It is a special time—these moments shared with your loved one—and it is made more valuable to both of you when you fully embody the present moment.

If you have ever done any kind of spiritual or mindfulness practice, your reading practice is similar to that. What I would add to this picture of mindfulness is a practice of study and research that is akin on a basic level to following good study habits and playing in a science lab. So while you are as aware of your thoughts, feelings, and sensory input as you would be with a mindfulness practice, at the same time you are developing two other "muscles": the skill of *finding* the essence of what you are communicating or reading, or of your co-creative activities, and the skill of *focusing* on that essence to gain a fuller understanding in order to transmit your learning to another, your loved one.

If you are reading to your loved one, you want to assimilate the meaning of the words as you read—really penetrate them by understanding and discerning the spiritual concepts and essence of what the author is communicating. When you are experiencing and exploring color, note not only how the color fills the paper, but also how a new color arises out of the combining of two colors. You will also be present to how each color makes you feel. If you choose to do a eurythmy practice, be in the imagination of the quality of the movement before ensouling the movement with your physical body.

With veil work, we are on the path of refining and improving our powers of concentration. If you find that while you're in service to your loved one, you suddenly lose the thread and realize you are thinking about the fact that you forgot to buy milk, gently come back and return your attention to your practice.

Three Soul Qualities: Reverence, Tenderness, and Gratitude

If you were preparing for a marathon, you would feed your body specific nutrients. Likewise, your soul is nourished by the activity of practicing specific qualities. You will find that practicing and cultivating *reverence*, *tenderness*, and *gratitude* in your daily life will strengthen your soul and prepare it to meet the spiritual world in the right way. This is an essential aspect of cultivating a welcoming mood. Let's take each of these in turn.

Reverence
Reverence includes qualities of honor, respect, awe, devotion, and veneration. If you are feeling separated from the quality of reverence, you might get reacquainted with it by looking back at your childhood and remembering a particular adult whom you admired. Reverence often arises in my soul when I admire someone whose qualities I would like to emulate in my own life. Today, prayer usually gets me in a place of practicing reverence: knowing that there is a power—God—that is greater than I am.

In his lecture The Mission of Reverence, Rudolf Steiner prescribes, "Love and devotion together make up reverence." In the same lecture he identifies the capacity of reverence both as a tool for connecting with the Divine (lifting the veil)—"The soul is

---

"Love and devotion together make up reverence."

---

drawn by the strength of its reverence towards the eternal, with which it longs to unite itself"—and a modern path of acquiring knowledge.[1] It follows that if we add reverence's ingredients of love and devotion to how we learn and understand truth, we can see truth from a larger perspective. I intuit from Steiner's teachings that reverence means having a firm sense of who we are and thinking and discerning the truth for ourselves (versus blindly following) while at the same time yielding to that Truth, to God, which is higher than ourselves.

Tenderness

Tenderness feels almost dangerous in our often harsh and cynical world. It requires us to remain awake in the moment, soften our hearts, and allow ourselves to be open and vulnerable—the reason it is such a valuable mood to bring to this work. When I think of tenderness I often recall the image of a delicate, soft rose or Raphael's painting *The Small Cowper Madonna*, an image of Mother Mary holding the infant Jesus. Tenderness is being soft, yes, but without being sappy. Underlying the quality of tenderness is a sense of fortitude.

Gratitude

For a time after my daughter's death, *gratitude* was not easy for me. If you are grieving deeply to the point where you feel only sadness and loss, and you can't seem to find your way toward gratitude, it's fine to let that go for now. I found a good beginning place for gratitude was being thankful that I had found the work of Rudolf Steiner, whose indications for working with the dead and whose information on the constructs of the spiritual world and what

---

*Underlying the quality of tenderness
is a sense of fortitude.*

---

happens when we die changed my life. Studying his work allowed me the opportunity to experience my relationship with my daughter and others who have crossed the threshold in a way that I never would have thought possible. With this practice you have the opportunity, whenever you wish, to continue your relationship with your loved one—helping them on their spiritual journey, as they help you. Working together you will lift us all up; you are co-creating a better world. When you immerse yourself in spiritual readings; spiritual thoughts, feelings, and activities, including color-rich images; and eurythmy movement, you are engaging in deeds that heal the soul. As your practice deepens you will find greater peace and renewal in how you approach and live your life. Your life will take unexpected twists and turns, as mine did, bringing unforeseen gifts and opportunities to learn new skills and meet new people. I trust you *will* find your way back to gratitude, which opens the heart to giving more and to receiving more.

Invite Your Angels

I know I have suggested inviting your angels to join you at the veil before, and this suggestion fits when you are cultivating a mood as well. In fact, it is always a good idea to bring them into your practice!

When you open to the extraordinary possibilities of connecting with the spiritual world, you also make yourself available to spiritual beings that can help and support you in your work. Who these are for you is an individual matter. For me, when I do my practice I invite the Christ, my personal angel, and Lara's angel.

Veil work is soulful work, and the most effective way to approach it is with a soulful presence.

At certain times I might also engage the guidance, strength, and courage of the Archangel Michael. Underutilized, benevolent spiritual beings are available to enhance our communication with our loved ones and to assist in our collaborative efforts. I am also grateful for their protection while doing this work. When we are dealing with what we cannot see, it's good to know that these beings have our highest good in mind and are interested only in moving us forward spiritually.

Veil work is soulful work, and the most effective way to approach it is with a soulful presence. Being a student of spiritual studies who is fully present, inviting the qualities of reverence and tenderness, feeling appreciative of life, and inviting help from the spiritual world are all ways to set the appropriate tone for offering your loved ones the spiritual nourishment they are seeking.

Veil Work Activities: Reverence, Tenderness, and Gratitude

I invite you to dedicate a page in your journal to each of these three "soul moods." Experiment with the following activities, and on each of these pages write out the activity that best cultivates each soul mood so you can come back to it later and practice again.

Reverence

- Make the eurythmy gesture for reverence: If you are able, stand upright, with soft knees. Come into the eurythmy gesture of reverence simply by crossing your arms over your chest, palms flat toward your chest and wrists touching. I prefer placing the left wrist on top of the right, but you can do it either way. Sense and note what your soul feels in the eurythmy gesture of reverence.

- Say the word "Hallelujah." Just saying this word is an act of reverence, of praising God. It is a Hebrew word meaning "praise ye YAH (Yahweh)." When Rudolf Steiner introduced the word to the eurythmists in the fall of 1912, he concluded the instruction with the words "Now you have done the word 'Halleluja.' This means, 'I purify myself from everything which hinders me from beholding the Highest.'"[2]

- Practice saying to a loved one, a friend, or—if you're really feeling adventurous—a stranger the word "namaste." Namaste is a Sanskrit word meaning "I bow to the Divine in you." How does it feel to recognize and acknowledge the Divine in another human being? Does it support you in cultivating a feeling of reverence for another?

- Take in a sunrise or sunset, or the view of the night's starry sky. Can you feel your heart and soul open to the feeling of reverence that the grandeur of such a sight invites?

Tenderness

A Color Exercise to Cultivate Tenderness

For this exercise you will work with magenta, the color of tenderness.

Gather the supplies you will need:

- 9" x 12" or 11" x 14" watercolor paper, or 60-pound drawing paper
- A 1-inch paintbrush (choose either goat hair or bristle versus nylon)
- Magenta watercolor pigment (Rose Madder hue/Winsor & Newton Cotman Watercolors—a brand of watercolors that is reasonably priced and easy to find)
- A paint pot or dish

Dilute the magenta paint with water in the paint pot or dish so that the paint becomes translucent. Place your paper vertically, or "portrait style," with the short edges at top and bottom. Start on the bottom left corner of your paper and slowly paint using long, slightly upward strokes from left to right. Make sure your strokes go all the way across the paper. After each stroke, lift the brush and start the next stroke from the left side of the paper. Gently breathe out with each stroke across the paper. Contemplate how your breathing has changed as you complete this exercise. Can you sense the feeling of tenderness gently awakening in your soul?

A Soul Gesture for Tender Intimacy

Rudolf Steiner gave indications for sixteen "soul gestures." Even though these soul gestures were originally given for doing poetry in eurythmy, we can all learn the feeling of the soul gesture by putting our body into one of these positions. Each gesture can suggest "the mood and feeling which may be called up within us by a poem taken as a whole."[3] By doing this eurythmy soul gesture, you can feel the soul quality of tenderness.

- Stand upright on the balls of your feet (the fleshy part of your foot) with your heels slightly off the ground (so slight you could slip only a piece of paper under them). Your knees are soft, hands at your sides.

- Gently hold out your arms in front of you, elbows bent, at about waist level.
- With your palms facing upward, touch your thumb and forefinger together on both hands.
- Contemplate Steiner's words about this gesture. "If you imagined to yourselves that you were holding a baby, and that you wanted to enter into a certain relationship with the guardian angel of this baby, you would hold it in this way, and you would then have the movement for Inwardness (Tenderness)."[4]

A Painting Contemplation for Tenderness

Find Raphael's painting *The Small Cowper Madonna* (an image of Mother Mary holding the infant Jesus) in a book or on the Internet. Practice feeling into this painting. Can you sense the quality of tenderness that Mary holds in her heart? See if you can discern a sense of awareness of her child's destiny—a tenderness that acknowledges Jesus's freedom to carry out his destiny.

Gratitude

- Try building your gratitude muscle daily. For five days in a row, write a list of five things that happen during your day that you are grateful for, big or small.
- Once a week write a handwritten note of gratitude to someone: a family member, friend, or professional colleague. In the note highlight how that individual is important and that the world is definitely a better place because they are in it.
- Notice how you feel before and after completing each gratitude exercise.

7

Reaching Through The Veil: Forms of Speaking

taying Connected: How to Continue Your Relationships with Those Who Have Died is a collection of lectures in which Rudolf Steiner gives specific indications on how to nurture and cultivate your relationship with your loved one. It is a book that I have read numerous times, making copious notes in the margins. I have underlined so many of the important sentences in the book that if I read it too many more times, I might just as well underline the whole book. Even though Steiner's lectures and books may be difficult to penetrate and understand, I highly recommend going straight to this source on communicating through the veil.

In this chapter and the next, I will share what I have learned from *Staying Connected* as well as what I have learned and experienced on my own in regards to how to set up a system of communication with your loved one who has died. You will develop a kind of vocabulary that the two of you will share. You will learn ways of "speaking" thoughts and feelings to your loved one, basic responses or messages that you can expect to receive, and optimum times to communicate. I will also give you a brief overview of the

----

*You will develop a kind of vocabulary
that the two of you will share.*

----

differences in communication when you are working with a child, an adult, and a person who has taken their own life.

The basic principle that underlies your communication with your loved one is that the two of you had a connection on Earth. It was one that could *only* be established and developed on Earth. It might be a connection through ancestry—a family bond. It could be a relationship forged through community, whether the community involves work and career, play, making music, or any other kind of group collaboration. The connection can also be made through a religious tradition or "spiritual stream" you share with people, whether or not you have physically met and even with those who lived in a different era but pursued the same spiritual path—provided your connection to that path was a deep and committed one. The common thread is that you had some kind of shared experience while living on this planet. The depth of your connection with the other will depend on the depth of the relationship you had with them, or with the spiritual stream you shared with them while living on Earth.

Speaking to Your Loved One Using Thoughts and Feelings

In the physical world we have all manner of discrete physical forms, from solid rock to plant life to human-made items to more fluid yet no less substantial forms of matter such as water—even a river is usually confined to its banks. It is easy for us to understand that rocks, plants, animals, and even human beings in the physical world

The spiritual world is in constant motion, with an expansive weaving together of living thoughts.

have a form: boundaries that separate one from the other. And with the exception of rocks, all will experience being dead at some point. What doesn't often come to mind, however, is that our *thoughts* can also be dead as viewed from a spiritual perspective. Our thoughts are dead when they are nonessential and materialistic. This kind of thinking is obviously needed to navigate in the physical world, but it has no relevance to the spiritual world.

Our materialistic thoughts aren't the only aspects of us that can be dead even while we continue to breathe in this physical life. Our feelings can also be dead—or maybe a more accurate term would be numb. In this hectic, overstimulated, and sometimes scary world, it makes sense that we would want to protect the most vulnerable part of ourselves: our heart center, home of our feelings. In an effort to protect ourselves we often deaden or numb our feelings by overconsuming everything from shopping to alcohol to food, sex, gambling, and more. We also overmedicate: fifty-two million people in the United States over the age of twelve have used prescription drugs *nonmedically* in their lifetime. The most abused of these are painkillers, tranquilizers, and stimulants.[1] All of these widespread efforts to numb and deaden are indicative of the fact that many of us are not able take hold of our feelings consciously. This means it is difficult for us to identify how we feel in the moment, which makes it hard to share our feelings with another.

The forms and boundaries in the spiritual world are of a different quality and therefore, in contrast to the physical world, the spiritual world is in constant motion with an expansive weaving together of *living* thoughts. Spiritual beings use these thoughts to create things that, depending on their spiritual content, will either hinder or enhance our spiritual evolution. To simplify, when you are communicating with the spiritual world, you want to keep this picture of continual movement and living creative activity in mind. It will remind you to make your communication both fluid and mobile. What that means for your practice is that you will learn to penetrate or infuse, as much as possible, your thoughts and feelings with a *living force*.

Create an Active Pictorial Image of Your Thought

This living force is active whenever we use our imagination to create an active pictorial image of our thoughts. It sounds easy, but it can be a little more challenging for us than it would at first seem. Because we have so much visual technology in our world today, we have lost some of our capacity to create imaginings or pictures of things. We have simply forgotten how to do it because we are too busy receiving images to create them ourselves. While it takes a certain amount of will and determination to actively create a "mini-movie" from a thought, I am asking you to do just that. The good news is that it's an innate human skill—we have tens of thousands of years of experience of it in our DNA in the form of storytelling, which requires us to create vivid images in our minds.

If you need some inspiration for cultivating this skill, read a biography of Albert Einstein, one of the shining examples of imaginative thinking in the modern era. Einstein preferred to think in pictures. As he once captured his thinking process, "I very rarely think in words at all." He later told a psychologist, "A thought comes, and I may try to express it in words afterwards."[2] Another model to study is Nikola Tesla, who would think through an entire invention before even beginning to construct it. As Marc Seifer writes in his biography of Tesla, "He could use his powers of visualization to mold his various creations, and even run and modify them in his mind, before committing them to paper and the material world."[3] And then there is Temple Grandin, author of *Thinking in Pictures: My Life with Autism*. Her imaginative capacity is enormous. She has deep rapport with animals and a PhD in animal science, and is architect of at least a third of the livestock-handling facilities in the United States. In her book she writes, "I think in pictures. Words are like a second language to me. I translate both spoken and written words into full-color movies, complete with sound, which run like a VCR tape in my head. When somebody speaks to me, his words are instantly translated into pictures."[4]

Instantly translating ideas into pictures, while adding the ingredient of warmth from our feeling life, is exactly what we strive for with veil work.

Deeply Penetrate the Thought You Want to Communicate

This particular skill is very relevant when you are doing the spiritual practice of reading to your loved one; attending spiritual lectures, church services, or other spiritual or religious gatherings; or watching a DVD with spiritual content. It means that you strive to understand the thinking behind what you are reading or hearing so well that you can explain it in your own words. The deeper your understanding of the thought, the more easily your loved one will receive it.

Warm Your Thought or Question with Genuine Feelings of Love, Interest, and Enthusiasm

Love
When I speak about warming your thought or questions with feelings of love, I'm referring to an objective love, selfless and unconditional,

---

*The love that warms your communication
is based on a devotional commitment
to be of service.*

---

one that does not desire or need personal gain to result from the communication. The love that warms your communication is based on a devotional commitment to be of service. A most beautiful, true role model of this form of love is depicted in Michelangelo's *Pietà*, depicting Mother Mary holding her adult son, Jesus, in her arms. This work of art reflects Christ's deed of love, but also the quality of love that we want to strive to emulate. Here we see Mary's unconditional love as she surrenders to the freedom of her child's destiny path. At the same time, she is fully present to her child's pain and suffering, knowing he had the power and greatness to have prevented what happened to him.

Interest

When we are deeply interested in the spiritual materials we are reading, or we deeply penetrate a question or thought we are sending to our loved one, we make it a *living* thing. A rote thought, by contrast—something we are simply reciting—is a dead thought. In addition to making the thought mobile, our interest builds a spiritual "substance," a potentiality that, when activated by the light of consciousness, helps us communicate. Interest is directly connected to our ability to listen. When we are interested, we lean into what we want to learn more about, so our listening skills perk up.

Marjorie Spock is known for being an inspiration for Rachel Carson's book *Silent Spring*. Spock was a well-known environmentalist and biodynamic gardener, in addition to being a eurythmist

*Enthusiasm adds a warm, golden glow,
a sun-kissed feeling, to your veil work.*

and author. In her little book *Group Moral Artistry: Reflections on Community Building*, she writes about the quality of listening, and I think provides valuable insight into the quality of interest that we want to develop with veil work.

Spock teaches that listening is an activity of opening up yourself to what lives in the person who is speaking. We humans are very good at thinking ahead. Who hasn't been in conversation and thinking what the other person is going to say next before they have even spoken the words? Yet if I am to really understand the person who is speaking, I must forget about my own concerns and agenda and give my attention to the other—or to apply this idea to veil work, give my attention to the spiritual content or thought I want to communicate.

Hopefully we all know what it feels like to *really* be listened to by another person. Spock writes that before we express our thought to someone else, that thought lies dormant within us. When we are being listened to, the same "substance" I mentioned earlier that is generated by interest is created, allowing the idea to grow, and now our conversation can bring many ideas to fruition. You can think of this essential, invisible substance as compost added to the gardener's soil, adding vitality and creative capacity.

If we take this teaching about listening and apply it to taking interest in spiritual content or thoughts, when we demonstrate interest we are "listening" for what the spiritual content is truly saying. The resulting substance that is created enables the spiritual idea to expand, allowing for more spiritual ideas to come to fruition.

Enthusiasm

Enthusiasm has an energy all its own. It is like sunshine on a bright summer day. It adds a warm, golden glow, a sun-kissed feeling, to your veil work. In eurythmy, the gesture for the zodiacal sign Leo embodies this quality of enthusiasm. The movement starts from your heart center, felt as a seed inside yourself, and then powerfully blossoms into the outside world. This is the strength of enthusiasm. It starts deep within you, and as it grows, the whole world can feel it.

Genuine enthusiasm and interest are two aspects of selfless love. This type of deep engagement doesn't wane when you do not get an immediate response or are met with what seems like silence from your loved one; rather, you are engaged for the duration. You remain inspired to keep bringing your question, thought, or spiritual content to them in a fresh and alive way, no matter what you receive in response.

Reversals

Reversals are messages from the spiritual world and are an important concept in veil work. At the same time, they can be hard to wrap your brain around. I put them in the area of my thinking where I know that the spiritual world does not look like the physical world, and that concepts like time and space as we know them aren't viable. In veil work we need to remain open to a different reality from the physical world we know.

That being said, I want to immediately contradict myself and explain reversals using the concepts of time and space. The first type of reversal occurs in space and comes as an image. I have not received many, but when I receive them it is always as I am coming out of sleep. And oh, what a thrill it is! In the next chapter I will give you an example of one of them.

The other type of reversal happens in time, and one example of reversals in time has to do with the conversation between ourselves and our loved one. With this type, the *sequence of a conversation is reversed*. What we say to our loved one is actually a thought or question that our loved one has placed in our soul. And what we think we have received from them is actually our own inner soul response that we are perceiving. So conversation in the flow of time is reversed. My thought "I love you, Lara" is a thought Lara placed in my soul, and her response, "I love you too, Mom," is my own soul response. We would normally perceive the conversation starting with us and traveling in time to our loved one, but that initiating conversation is actually coming back toward us in time. As another example, let's say a question arises in my soul: "I wonder how my mother is doing?" Utilizing this reversal concept, my mother is placing that question in me. If I receive back the image of her hands placed on my cheeks and her looking at me with love, this is my response back to my mother—I am giving her my love. I use these types of messages to slow down and stop for a moment. It might be a moment of exchanging love, or it might be a moment when I get information from my mother.

I use the reversal concept in my veil work practice simply by having awareness of it. But I can't say it is something I am overly precise about. Most of the time there seems to be a natural flow to my conversations with my loved ones, and usually when I have received a thought or feeling that is clearly out of the blue, I already have a knowingness that it came from them.

Until you get used to the natural flow of conversation across the veil, you might simply try being conscious that when a question or thought rises up in you and you want to communicate it to your loved one, they might actually have placed it there.

Stuart Wilde (1946–2013) was a spiritual seeker, author, and international speaker who talks about reversals in several of his books, especially the mirrorlike symmetry of the physical world in relation to the spiritual world. In his book *Sixth Sense: Including the Secrets of the Etheric Subtle Body,* Wilde suggests a connection between reversals and the optic part of the brain. I think this is worth considering when we try to understand the mystery of reversals. Wilde writes,

This idea is not so daft, for when we look at something via normal sight, we perceive it the right way up; however, we know that that image reaches us upside down, twisted left to right. There is a mechanism in the brain that turns reality's images around for us, so we see the room we are in, for example, the right way up. However, perhaps information from our senses reaches the subconscious in its original upside-down, twisted right-to-left state, instead of our how our normal waking perception sees and perceives reality.

Note that the right-to-left state corresponds nicely to reversals in time, and the upside-down image relates spatially. Wilde goes on to say, "If the subconscious is symmetrically aligned to the spirit worlds, then one could quite confidently argue that it is a part of those worlds, and that a part of us is perpetually in the spirit world via our subconscious—not just after death, but also while we are still alive."[5]

Use Verbs Instead of Nouns

Abstract thoughts can exist only within the head's dead thinking; they fall away together with the physical body that is left behind. Thus the dead ... have no connection with nouns, the most abstract parts of speech. They can still live in verbs, for these are filled and carried by a soul-motion in which they can participate. Above all, they perceive what is spoken out of feeling.[6]

While I have found pictorial images most effective in reaching through the veil, I often use words to frame a question, comment, or thought, especially if I am recording a dialogue in my journal. It is important to know that our loved ones will lose the capacity to understand the meaning of a noun before they will lose their understanding of verbs. This goes back to the quality of continual

*Verbs are the liveliest, most active words
in our language, carrying the quality of movement.*

movement and flux in the spiritual world. Verbs are the liveliest, most active words in our language, carrying the quality of movement. Nouns—persons, places, or things—on the other hand, are formed and fixed in space. Know, too, that eventually our loved ones will lose all connection with language as we know it and will communicate only via thoughts or feelings.

A simple example of using verbs is the word "color." If you wanted to ask your loved one if they would like to color, instead of thinking the noun "color" and holding an image of crayons in your mind, you would use "coloring" as a verb and create an image of the two of you coloring together. Personally, I find it helpful to write down the words that help me create the most lively picture or image. For example, I might ask, "Do you want to *study* and *play* (verbs) with the colors of the rainbow, or would you rather *read* and *learn* (verbs) about the tasks of the spiritual hierarchies?" Then I warm the words and the image of these activities by infusing them with how I feel about doing them with my loved one: for example, *joy*.

As another example, if you are asking your loved one to help you select a book to read, instead of asking, "What book (noun)?" and picturing a static image of a book, I suggest you reframe both your question and the image you hold in your mind: "What book shall we *read* (verb)?" while holding the image of the two of you deeply engaged in reading. Sometimes for me this takes the form of an image of Lara holding up a book so I can see the cover.

Most of us don't stop to think about whether a word we're speaking is a noun or a verb—we're simply not trained to do it. But this is part of reaching through the veil. It will take a little practice, but it will quickly pay off by making your communication much more effective. Your journal will help you with this process of clarifying your thoughts and shaping your questions and is an excellent way to observe the most effective patterns in your communication with your loved ones. It is a wonderful tool for this purpose.

Work with Spiritual Content

Because those who have died no longer have physical organs of perception—eyes and ears, for example—they remember what *material* thoughts are for only a short time after their death, which is why, while they are in the spiritual world, it is easiest for your loved ones to find you when you think *spiritual* thoughts. Spiritual content is enlightened—*lit up* and discernable in the spiritual world. When your thoughts are anchored in Spirit, I invite you to imagine yourself, every cell of your body, literally shining and glowing. Or to use another image, see yourself as switching on the lights on a dark runway: now you have made it crystal clear to a pilot landing a plane at night where to touch down.

Your dedicated practice of reading spiritual content has the same effect, illuminating you to your loved one. And this can take place in "mini-moments" too, whenever you consciously focus on a spiritual thought you enjoy meditating on. This could be a line from a prayer, a spiritual poem, a mantra, or a phrase from scripture. What is important is that it reflects a spiritual truth. Here are three sentences I have used over the years:

I radiate God's loving Light.
Not I, but the Christ in me.
In the Beginning was the Word.

Choosing When to Communicate with Your Loved One

You can create questions or messages for your loved ones and communicate with them at any time throughout the day. However, I have found three optimal times for delivering my communication, and I strongly encourage you to take advantage of these times when the veil is especially thin.

- During the magical time as you fall asleep, holding your question, thought, or image for as long as you can, right to the moment of sleep.
- During your reading practice. You can do this just before you begin your practice, during it, or at the end. I have done all three.
- During times you intentionally set aside to talk with your loved one. You can do this on your daily walk, while journaling, or when participating in spiritual or artistic activities (color work, music, movement, playing, and study).

Veil Work Activities

My intention for you with the following activities is that you begin to stretch the "muscles" that will support you in your communications with your loved one.

Imaging

Go to your journal and find the page(s) where you listed sensory images of your loved one. I invite you to take one of the memories you listed and build up that single sensory image—one memory at a time—in your mind. And as you do that, bring movement into the picture.

I will share an example, walking you through how I might build up a memory of a time when Lara, her father, and I visited a waterfall.

Re-create the environment.

It is a warm, sunny day and I can hear the ten-foot waterfall softly splashing into the small pool of water below. I am sitting on the bank, where I can feel the coolness of the waterfall and the shade of the trees around us.

What can you hear?

In addition to the sound of the waterfall, Lara and her dad are laughing as they splash up out of the water.

What action is taking place?

I have a warm beach towel ready to wrap Lara up in. As I envelop Lara in the blanket, I can feel her shivering and giggling at the same time. I can see her broad smile.

What can you feel?

I am still wet from when I was in the water with them, so when I pull Lara close to me we are both wet. I can feel the weight of her small body, and yet there is a strength about it at the same time. It is a joy-filled moment. I feel blessed.

Now write about a memory of your own, using my prompts and creating your own additional ones to strongly bring back that memory of a time spent with your loved one. Note your new prompts in your journal.

Re-creating a Moment of Enthusiasm

Bring to mind a time when you felt enthusiastic about something or someone. What were the elements of that experience? Did it start as a small seed in your heart center? How did your enthusiasm naturally expand out to others without your having to do anything—but be enthusiastic! Write about your enthusiasm in your journal.

Playing with Reversals

Here are four ways to cultivate experiences of a reversal:

On a piece of unlined paper, write your name horizontally. On the same line, continue writing your name but write it backward, the reverse image. If you need help with this, write out your name and hold it up to a mirror; you will see the reverse image you want to duplicate. However, first try doing it without a mirror.

Now spell your name out loud and then spell it out loud backward: Lynn/nnyL. Try other words and word sequences. See how fast you can get.

Create an image of a sphere or cube in your mind. At one point on the sphere, or corner of a cube, start to turn the sphere or cube inside out. If necessary, you can practice this kind of exercise with a real sock. Start with a point on the seam where the toes meet and turn the sock inside out from that point. Once you see how it works, then practice turning the sock inside out using only your imagination—picture images.

Draw an image in your mind of a five-pointed star, starting at the top of the star. Now retrace the lines of the star, erasing them as you go. Do this as fast as you can and as many times as you can. I often do this exercise if I have a hard time falling asleep at night. Note: it may help to draw it on paper first. Again starting with the top of the star, draw a straight line to the bottom right point, a straight line to the upper left point, a straight line horizontally across to the right point, and a straight line to the bottom left point. The fifth line returns home to the original starting point. Now retrace it.

Practice Asking a Question

Practice writing out a question to ask your loved one. Create a living image to accompany it that is sensory filled and would connect your loved one to you. Hint: always include at least their first name.

Examples: _____ , what book would you like to read together? _____ , what are you doing? _____ , how can I be of service to you?

Further Reading

Staying Connected, How to Continue Your Relationships with Those Who Have Died by Rudolf Steiner, Anthroposophic Press, 1999.

Group Moral Artistry: Reflections on Community Building by Marjorie Spock, St. George Publications, 1983.

8

Receiving Through The Veil: Forms of Seeing and Listening

It must be said that our social, ethical, and religious lives would be endlessly enriched if the living allowed themselves to be advised by the dead.
—Rudolf Steiner[1]

I would ask for a message, and the spirit would say something like, "I know life is hard, mate, but it will all be okay in a couple of months or so, and don't forget, God loves ya." Having delivered a constant stream of relatively inane messages over a period of six months or so, I came to the conclusion that if you are thick as two planks when you are alive, you are thick as two planks when you are dead.
—Stuart Wilde[2]

*B*oth of the quoted teachings are important to keep in mind as we communicate with our loved ones. Yes, we have a huge opportunity as well as a responsibility to learn from our loved ones who have died, *and* messages also come through that are less than helpful. Many of us, myself included, desire to receive communication through the veil. Yet I don't know too many folks—in fact I know of no one—with the level of initiatory skills Steiner had. We are likely to fall short in our ability to "hear" communication across the veil with accuracy and to know that the message is valid. In fact, because of our enthusiasm and genuine interest in this work, many of us can be easily misled or can misconstrue or misunderstand the messages we receive. Personally, I am willing to take the risk that I will not hear correctly or will misunderstand. I have had enough experiences of messages being clear and on target by now that I know it is worth continuing to be open to receive.

The ways we receive messages from our loved ones can vary just as much as the ways we send them, and to help illustrate this I am going to go into some detail in this chapter, including a few stories about how I have received communication myself.

To increase your skill in being receptive to and understanding communication from those who have died, you can add three activities to your practice:

- Consciously engage your angel. As you learned earlier, we all have a special angel that is "assigned" to us—what many people would call their guardian angel, or guiding angel. Ask your angel to support you in seeing and understanding what your loved ones need and their purpose in engaging with you.
- Practice feeling as if your loved one is looking at you, because in most cases when we do this work, they are. Just as we observe things that are outside ourselves—there is my coffee mug, there is a tree, there is my friend—so they observe us. The exception is with children who have died; we practice observing them.

The ways we receive messages from our loved ones can vary just as much as the ways we send them.

- Consistently record data. It's helpful to have a journal or note-book in the place where you read to your loved one, on your nightstand, and in your car. I cannot tell you how many times I have wished I were more disciplined in organizing my spiritual research. It is extremely rewarding and fruitful to look back at the techniques our loved ones have used to communicate and the content they wish to share with us. Over time, the patterns of their communications will reveal themselves to you. You will begin to see where they might be in their soul's journey as well as their areas of spiritual interest.

What kinds of experiences will you note in your journal? Following are just a few of the ways you may hear from the spiritual world.

A Thought or Feeling Pops into Your Awareness That Clearly Does Not Originate from You

How can you tell whether a thought or feeling is yours or not? You have undoubtedly had the experience of a random thought popping into your head, or of rehashing a thought over and over again. Sometimes you just get a funny feeling. Thoughts and feelings that come from your loved ones typically prompt a specific action—or a decision not to act in some cases—that has an effect. These can range from seemingly insignificant to life altering.

After Lara died and several months into my reading practice with my loved ones, I received a thought that activated my will: to color in my daughter's coloring book. This thought arrived with a subtle but definite force. I felt compelled to get up out of my chair, get Lara's crayons and coloring book, and sit down again to color. It was a "simple" act, but that was the beginning of my study of the spiritual nature of color, which opened me up to a whole new dimension of ways to experience color. In fact, I became an artist and sold many of my paintings at art shows. It was very clear to me at the time that the thought to pick up Lara's crayons was not mine, and the fact that it started me on a course of study I had never even heard of before only reinforced that conclusion.

Or you might have a strong feeling. After Lara's death I was blessed in that my husband was working full time, which allowed me the space to heal. I spent my time working in our garden and reading spiritual materials to Lara and other loved ones. Outside of exploring the spiritual aspects of color through self-study and an occasional art class, I was not engaged in any form of grief therapy. Yet I started to have the feeling that I needed to do something with a more outward focus, not just be contemplative and in my own world. I was not sure what to do, but I definitely knew that going back to the corporate world I was fully immersed in when Lara was born was not "it."

I saw a eurythmy performance that was quite lovely, and later came to find out that there was a therapeutic component to this movement form. Because I enjoyed movement in general, and I knew eurythmy was a spiritually based movement, I thought I would try a therapeutic eurythmy session. I was hopeful that it would help me get clarity on what type of work I could do for the "rest of my life." I booked a session. It was February 2001.

My first therapeutic eurythmy session was with Truus Geraets, a feisty yet wise therapeutic eurythmist. This session led me in a direction I had never imagined—I never expected that I would end up going to eurythmy school myself. And I never actually had that thought: *Yes, go to eurythmy school.* It was always a feeling, a feeling that said, *Take it day by day. It is important that you do this. We will be with you.* That feeling formed the underlying foundation that carried me through seven years of training. I know that feeling was not mine—it was a feeling Lara placed in me.

It is easier to discern whether a thought or feeling is your own when you have a certain level of self-knowledge, and as with everything in this work, it is a matter of practice. Further along I will describe a Daily Review practice that I have found helpful in cultivating the skill of observing my thoughts and feelings and learning to understand and know their source. Thoughts and feelings can develop from your own personal experiences or can be messages from your loved ones, who are always working to support and add to what you are trying to create in the world. Learning to tell the difference is part of this practice.

In fact, another way to cultivate this capacity is to consider the possibility that few thoughts you have are actually of your own making. Yes, I am asking you to consider that many of your thoughts are placed in your stream of consciousness by loved ones who have died and/or spiritual beings. I have come to realize that my best thoughts, ideas, and inspirations come from these sources.

You Might Receive a Message for Someone Else

The other morning during my reading practice, my Grandma Rollins came forward to talk with me. To give you a little background, while I was growing up, Grandma Rollins was not a relative I felt particularly connected with. It's not that I didn't love her, but she was a tad stern, and so as a child, I was a little afraid of her. She died when I was in college, and I never really knew her as an adult. Despite the fact that we were never close, over the years I have always included her in my thoughts as I do my spiritual reading practice, and in the last year or so she has become more vocal.

I was doing my reading session on my living room sofa instead of at the kitchen table this particular morning. All of a sudden, the thought *Grandma Rollins* came into my head and interrupted my reading. I received a thought from her that told me she was at the other end of the sofa, while at the same time an image of her formed in my mind. She was dressed in the same style of dress as when I last remember seeing her: sleeves just above her elbows (she always wore dresses) and her hair fixed in a short bob style that grandmothers wore in the seventies and that accented her naturally wavy hair. I could see the wrinkles on her face and the wire-rimmed glasses sitting on her nose. Typical of Grandma Rollins, there was no beaming smile; instead, she had an "I am here to do business" manner—not in a mean way, but in Grandma's way. It was actually very sweet, and I was not at all afraid of her presence. In fact, it felt quite normal to perceive her this way.

I acknowledged her by saying aloud while holding this image, "Hi, Grandma." Then I paused, with a feeling of anticipation. "Is there something I can do for you?"

Grandma Rollins delivered these thoughts into my mind as I held steady the image of her at the end of the sofa:

Thank you for all that you did for Uncle Bill. (My Uncle Bill died in January 2013, and my siblings and I were there to assist him through the passage of death and then afterward handled his estate. It was now May 2015.)

"You are welcome," I said. She continued:

I want you to tell your brother Rick that I really appreciate what he did on behalf of Billy. He treated him with respect and dignity.

Okay, I thought. I felt a firmness about her request that ignited my will. I decided to pop my brother an email right then and there. I rose from the sofa, went to my computer, and did just that, telling

Rick what I thought I understood my grandmother to say. I had not gotten the message exactly right, but it turned out that I was close. The following is our correspondence:

Howdy Rick,

I have felt Grandma Rollins's presence strongly over the last year or so. I never felt really close to her and wasn't sure why I would feel her around me. Finally I settled on the thought that maybe, because she was a teacher, she was wanting to help me on the Easing Grief project and now the book that I am writing. However, just now I felt her again and got the distinct impression that she wanted to say "Thank you" to me for being with Bill when he died. And I also got the strong message that she wanted to make sure that you knew how much she appreciated that you were with him and all that you did to make his transition from the physical world to the spiritual world more comfortable and one with human dignity.

Love,

Lynn

Hi Lynn,

*Thank you for the note. It is funny that I am still dealing with Uncle Bill's grave marker. **Just got it resolved.** [My emphasis] Long story ... I can share when we are together in July. Attached is the marker for Grandma and Grandpa. They are going to add Bill's name to it.*

Love,

Rick

I had no idea that my brother was still working, more than two years later, on my Uncle Bill's grave marker. But considering the timing of her message to me, I'm sure that Grandma Rollins knew.

A Message Comes from Your Living Child

I have a wonderful example of how this can happen. Having met through our common interest in Rudolf Steiner's work, Kim and I have known each other for more than ten years. Kim met the actress Mala Powers in 2002, five years before Mala died. Even though the two of them only shared a short few years together, they had a remarkable bond that was deeper than their common interest in acting. In fact, I think Kim could write an entire book about the spiritual connections that have woven through both of their lives. One of the stories Kim shared with me was about her son, Donny, who was born after Mala died. At age two and a half, Donny already knew of Mala from photos and stories that Kim had shared with him. One morning at a time when Kim was under quite a bit of stress and in need of some emotional support, her very young son woke up and told her, "I played with Grandma Mala in heaven." Then Donny put his hand on Kim's cheek and tilted his head in a gesture just like a familiar one of Mala's and very clearly said, "Oh, my sweet girl, you are doing just fine."

A Message Comes Through a Dream or a Dreamlike Vision

I will use an example to illustrate this kind of communication as well. Lara and her kindergarten speech teacher, Donna, had a deep connection with each other. I still remember when the two of them met. Warm smiles lit up their faces as they said hello; it was like the recognition of two souls who had known each other from a previous life. Even after we moved from Pennsylvania, where the two met, to California, we stayed in touch with Donna.

When Lara died, Donna was unable to fly to California for the funeral, and this was very distressing for her because she loved Lara dearly. Donna later wrote to me about her experience. This is a lengthy passage, but I find it so beautiful and the detail is so wonderful that I include it in its entirety:

It had become late and Bill had gone to bed. I needed some time to myself so I stayed up and looked through my collection of pictures of Lara. It felt somewhat comforting to recall the memories of our times together here in Pennsylvania—but this constant distraction of getting to California seemed to override any reprieve I was feeling. I had never experienced such torment. Emotionally drained, I decided to try to get some sleep—still not knowing for sure what I would or could do about coming for the funeral.

Sleep did not come easily. I found myself dozing fitfully and consumed with an unusual restlessness. Despite my anxiety, I apparently succumbed to a deeper state of pure exhaustion.

What took place during the remainder of the night is still a bit of a mystery to me for I simply do not know what to call it. For lack of a better word, I will refer to it as a dream—yet, its reality, its vividness, its impact upon my senses were all different and certainly heightened by comparison to any other dream I have ever experienced.

The first thing that I recall was that I had been walking for a very long time on a beautifully barren beach. No one was in sight, yet the solitude was only slightly comforting. I could literally "feel" the warmth from the morning sun on my face as a mild breeze gently coaxed the lapping waves ashore. The only sounds were those of the sea and its gulls. Although enveloped in this tranquil setting, my mind was not at all at peace. My sadness was overwhelming and my anxiety from not being with you brought an actual ache to my chest. The tears that clouded my eyes brought about a misty appearance to all that I saw.

I continued across the sand until I reached a jetty formed of massive rocks. As I climbed upward I was thinking back to when I was a child and had played on a similar formation on a New England beach at about the same age as Lara. Upon reaching the top, I was startled out of my "flashback" by two seagulls as they gracefully flew above me and into the direction from which I had just come. As I turned to follow their flight, my gaze was drawn to the sand I had previously walked upon.

There in that beautiful stretch of beach was the impression of my footsteps, and paired right beside mine another very clear, yet smaller set of prints—step for step—like those of a child.

Then before I even had time to contemplate where and how these tiny steps appeared, I heard what was unmistakably, undeniably Lara's voice, calling my name. She said it only once, but I knew it was her voice. My body turned to follow that sweet sound and then I saw her.

She appeared almost suspended, her feet not quite touching the rocks. She was dressed in pink, although the detail of the dress was unclear. Her hair was tied in a wide satin ribbon off to one side with little blondish wisps, almost transparent looking, blowing in the soft breeze. My heart raced at the sight as I witnessed how healthy and oh, so lovely, her body looked. Slowly she held out her hands and lifting one as if to wave, she quietly whispered, "It's okay."

Although barely audible, the sweet sound of those words went through my entire body. She was beyond beautiful, smiling with that "rascally" sparkle in her eye (you know the look). I smiled back, speechless—knowing I needed not to speak. I just suddenly knew she was safe and healthy and happy! Wanting so much to touch her, I stepped forward, reaching out to her ...

I awakened at that moment to find myself sitting upright in bed, arms extended. It was 4 a.m. I remember feeling a bit sad that the "dream" had ended, yet I also felt something much more powerful—an incredible sense of peace had replaced the anguish of needing to be in California. Don't misunderstand, I still wanted to be with you but the "necessity" was removed. I "felt" Lara's message—it was okay. It was as if we were *both unburdened, she from her unhealthy body and I from my torment.*

As I looked around the room, the glow from the moonlight shining through our skylight had illuminated the framed poem that Tracy [Donna's daughter] had given me. The poem "Footprints" was one my mother carried with her at all times. I immediately thought of the ironic connection with my dream and actually smiled at the fact that this might be one of those signs you so often speak of. It wasn't until later when you told me you had chosen that very same poem for Lara's prayers cards that it really struck me! And I could hear you saying, "There are no coincidences."

This is an exceptional example of a message that comes through in a dream or a dreamlike state. If Donna had only experienced a fragment of this—perhaps just Lara's voice saying, "It's okay"—it would have been a wonderful example. So as you are evaluating the messages you receive, know that they can be very simple or more involved. Your loved ones have many ways to make their presence known.

Note, too, that the message here came in images, a theme of the footsteps prayer that Donna was familiar with. This is not unusual, for our loved ones will often place their messages within images we are comfortable with. How loving of them.

A Message Comes After Extensive Biographical Study

My colleague Sylll Vie recently shared several experiences of co-creation she had with someone who died in 1999.

While she was completing her master's in education, one of her assignments was to study the biography of a deceased individual whose life's work she felt aligned to, someone she could relate to as a patron. The name M. C. Richards came into her consciousness—through the back door, so to speak, as a whisper.

Richards, as it turned out, was a very intense, creative, free, and bold individual who did not want to be defined by one sphere of activity—she was variously a poet, a potter, a painter, a teacher, and a farmer. Her lively qualities filled Sylll Vie with a buoyant energy that came through when it was time to do a presentation about her, and even the ideas for the content of the presentation seemed to be following Richards's lead. Sylll Vie remained open to these ideas and impulses throughout the experience.

Sylll Vie continued her studies and another impulse from Richards became clear when she was moved to explore self-portrait painting. She felt guided by Richards through the entire exercise; it felt like artistic dialogue and "play time" with M. C.!

M. C. Richards is still not through with Sylll Vie. She has also influenced her to change the subject of her thesis to be more aligned with who she now is: an artist. The subject now is the teacher as artist—the ways in which understanding the creative artistic process can help in the activity of teaching.

To me, what is most notable about Sylll Vie's co-creative experience is that the messages took the form of an inner hearing clearly not initiated by her. Even though there is a feeling of freedom in saying no to such an impulse, there is a greater feeling that comes with taking on the responsibility to listen and follow through with what the person who has died is asking for, for the greater good.

A Message Comes Through
Another Person, an Animal, or a Sign

Through Another Person

Over my years of doing veil work, I have become much more attuned to the people I interact with every day and what my meeting with another person looks like. When you probe your interactions at the end of each day, you can ask yourself some very useful questions to find out whether aspects of them were especially significant. Where was the meeting? Was it a random meeting? Was there an overriding feeling within the meeting itself? What was the conversation about? Was there something different about the communication that stands out for you?

I am reminded of an experience I had during my second year of eurythmy school. My class had just finished our artistic performances for the end of term. The overall mood at the school was jovial as we had all met another milestone on our path to graduation and receiving our diplomas. To get to this point it had taken me four and a half years of part-time training, commuting back and forth on a fairly regular basis from my California home to New York, where the school campus was located. Now, if I continued the training, I would have to live on campus and join the full-time training for the remaining two years; I could go home only at the Christmas holiday and during summer break.

At the age of fifty-two it was a difficult decision for me to make. Not only was the training itself demanding, but the commitment to finish required me to relinquish much of what I felt was my personal freedom. Several of my close classmates knew that it was a hard decision for me.

A pivotal moment occurred that evening with Kanako, the school's eurythmy pianist. After the performances that evening she walked up to me out of the blue and said, "It is very important to your daughter that you continue going to school."

It was a very powerful and meaningful interaction. It was as though my daughter was telling me, through Kanako, to see the training through to completion and receive my diploma. Even though Kanako could have learned of Lara from my fellow students, I could recall no conversation with Kanako about my daughter or about being at such a crossroads in my eurythmy training.

Through Animals

Just as we humans can manipulate physical objects, our loved ones who have died can manipulate animals. I believe there is a very real correlation between the rise of people's interest—and in some cases a mild obsession—with animals and the fact that now is the time for us to fully serve and collaborate with those who have died. It's as though we know this at a deep spiritual level but now have to bring it to a conscious knowing.

When Lara was alive, we lived in an open-concept home where the family room, dining room, and kitchen area were all open to one another. We had sectioned off a space and made it into Lara's play/learning center and filled it with books, toys, and pillows. About a week or so after Lara's death, a friend phoned to say hello. While we were talking I looked over at Lara's area, and on top of one of her pillows I saw a mouse. It was simply sitting still there.

"Wow, that's weird," I said to my friend. "I don't remember Lara having a stuffed mouse—Oh, my gosh, I have to hang up. That's a *real* mouse!"

The mouse was facing toward the big sliding-glass doors that lined one of the walls. I don't like mice. At all. But for some reason, I was able to walk calmly to the door and open it. And I said to the mouse, which was about five feet away from the open door, "Out," as I gestured that direction with my arm.

Not only did the mouse not go out the door, but it actually got up, turned 180 degrees to face away from the door, and then proceeded to sit back down on my daughter's soft pillow. I could not believe it. I phoned my husband and said, "Please come home. There is a mouse sitting on Lara's pillow."

That morning my husband was working about an hour away from home, and he asked me, sensibly enough, "Don't you think the mouse will have moved by the time I get there?"

For some reason, I needed him home. I asked him again, and Butch, sensing my need for him and as kind as he was, said he would.

I sat with the mouse for an hour—and neither of us moved.

When my husband arrived at the sliding door and peered in to find the mouse sitting on the pillow facing me, the look of pure astonishment on his face was priceless. He was very strategic about what he did next. He went to the pantry, grabbed a cylindrical pasta container, and emptied the spaghetti. Then he walked over to the mouse and placed the container on its side in front of the animal. The mouse got up off the pillow and walked right into the container. Then the two of us walked out to the field by our home and he let it go.

It's hard to explain why, but our response to one small mouse having been in Lara's play area was to pull that part of the room completely apart, even tearing up the area rug and disposing of it. By early evening we had made it into a beautiful space with a bookshelf that displayed several of Lara's favorite books and a couple of other items that were special to us.

As we were setting up the new area, my husband disclosed to me that it had been painful to come home from work and see Lara's space without her and me there reading a book or playing. With Butch's words I began to understand the reason for the mouse's appearance and its odd behavior. I appreciated the mouse's gift, although at that time I didn't know it had come from one of my loved ones who had died.

When mice come into my life, I pay attention. I don't think it was my daughter who manipulated that particular mouse, but it might have been my mother. Two other incidents that have happen since that first one lead me to think this. What I do know is that there is a definite pattern when mice appear in my life: a loved one is telling me it is time to let go of something.

I have also received messages through hummingbirds, feathers, and once even the tail of a gray squirrel on my front porch. I expect there will be more. I invite you to pay special attention whenever you have an unusual encounter with an animal.

Through Signs

Signs come in all shapes, sizes, and forms. They could be literal human-made signs like license plates or billboards. They could be natural events that hold meaning, such as wind or rain, or the sudden appearance of a rainbow or shooting star.

I am not quite sure how these signs are manifested, especially the human-made ones. For instance, there was what happened on my daughter's last school day in Pennsylvania before we moved to the Los Angeles area. Lara had touched many people there. As we pulled out of the parking lot that day, the license plate on the car in front of us read, "LUV U CAM"—which I read as Love You Came. It was a sweet good-bye message. Most likely our loved one engages the help of our angels and other spiritual beings, but I really don't know—it's one of the many mysteries we can explore further. But signs like this happen often and do get my attention when I see them.

Natural events like shooting stars and rainbows make more sense to me, probably because stars and rainbows are filled with spirit and spiritual beings. After my father died, the majesty of a full double rainbow against the backdrop of the San Diego Mountains graced my three siblings and me while we were driving from the memorial service to his gravesite. It has now become part of our family lore and a reminder of our father. My brother David wrote my siblings and me of his adventures in Tanzania, where he was preparing to climb Mount Kilimanjaro, and ended his email this way: *p.s.: pretty cool double rainbow from Dad the first night I arrived!*

A friend told me about how she learned of her grandmother's death. She received the news on a quiet night in the desert, far from streetlights and buildings. Sighing, she looked up at the heavens to see a brilliant shooting star streaking across the sky, and she thought, *Oh! There she goes!*

Through Reversals

We explored reversals in the last chapter, but it's appropriate to bring them up here too. Reversals—images appearing backward—usually come to me upon awakening. My strongest reversal message came a couple of years after Lara's death. I had taken into my sleep the question "Lara, what are you doing?" In the magical moment of coming out of sleep, I received an image of a small child in a white garment standing at an easel with a paintbrush in her hand. It was a familiar image; I had seen a painting of that very same image at my sister's home. Later that day, I phoned my sister. Although it was no longer hanging on the wall, she remembered the picture; it was now rolled up in the basement. I asked her if she could mail it to me. When I unrolled it I discovered that not only was it the same image that had come to me as I woke up, but it was a *reverse* of the image I received upon waking. I had seen the little girl facing right but in the painting, she faced left. Now of course, in the spiritual world they don't have paintbrushes and easels—that was not what Lara was literally doing. But to me the message was clear: Lara was working on exploring colors, and I knew I was on the right track by serving her through studying the spiritual nature of colors.

Electronic Signs

For me the jury is out regarding the messages I have received through electronic means, mainly through the telephone and emails. Still, things have happened that are hard to explain. For example, Doris, my mother's name, is not a common name these days, but at certain times over the years I have had messages both for and from "Doris" left on my phone answering machine. Email messages are also curious. Recently a friend of mine received a "spam" email from her deceased mother, with her mother's full name in the sender address saying: "Hi! How are you?"

I can recommend a couple of things to do if you receive an electronic message. You could take the question into your sleep: "(Name), is there something that I can help you with?" or "(Name), are you wanting something from me?" Or explore where your loved one is during the time that they are spending in "Kamaloka." We will discuss this time period in more detail in chapter 17. But briefly, we spend a third of the timespan of our earthly life after we die in the spiritual realm of Kamaloka, and we experience it backward, taking one year to review three years of our life. If your loved one was sixty years old when they died, and you received a message from them five years after they died, you can expect them to be reviewing their life at about the age of forty-five: three times five years = fifteen years, and sixty minus fifteen = forty-five. With this as a reference point in time, look at your relationship with your loved one when they were forty-five years old. Was there something significant going on during that time? If so, that might give you a clue as to what they might want to contact you about.

Favorable Moments to Anticipate Responses from Your Loved Ones

I have observed a pattern in the times when I am most likely to receive communication from my loved ones. Be especially aware of thoughts, feelings, and signs at these times:

- The magical time right as you are waking out of sleep
- During your reading practice or when you are journaling
- When your mind is not particularly focused on anything—for example, when you are driving. (Hint: keep a little notebook in your car to record your experiences.)
- On the anniversary of their birth or death date
- Certain times of the year such as holidays or festivals that hold special shared memories for you and your loved one

Communication Differences in Special Death Situations

Children Versus Adults

The human being has three primary soul force activities: thinking, feeling, and willing. Our willing is manifested through our actions, our behavior. Our ego personality, that part of us that says "I am," is strongly connected to thinking and the memories we have created in our lifetime. When we die and shed our physical body, as difficult as it is to imagine, these three soul forces start to separate. Our thinking disengages first and journeys out to the spiritual worlds ahead of our feelings and will. We will talk more about this when we discuss the soul's journey after death. For now, what is important to understand is that normally, the child who dies has yet to develop their full thinking capacities and has not yet created a treasure chest of a lifetime of memories. Because of this, the child's thinking is not fully developed at the point of death. When you consider this, you can understand why Rudolf Steiner suggests that we enter into a relationship with a child who has died primarily through our feelings.

Steiner indicates that when we are developing a relationship with a child who has died, we create an imagination of what it was like to play together.[3] We engage the feelings we had when we met the child in play. When we feel sadness or pain about their death, it is often the pain they feel from not being able to be with us physically. By feeling this sadness in our own souls, we help ease this pain for them, or are at least able to share the pain with them. He recommends the thoughts we communicate with them be universal in nature. *Love thy neighbor as thyself* is an example of a universal thought. In contrast, with an adult we create a connection through thought-filled memories of their life and contributions that they made.

I believe that the fact that children have not fully developed their thinking capacity is behind Rudolf Steiner's statement "When

---

*Be especially aware of thoughts, feelings,
and signs that come through at the magical time
as you are waking out of sleep.*

---

children die in early life they continue to be with us, spiritually with us....We do not lose little children, for they remain more or less within the sphere of earthly humanity."[4] I experience Lara's inspirations through my feelings, whether they take the form of an impulse to connect with her father or to explore a spiritual topic to study. Certainly, my feelings told me to enter and complete eurythmy training. Even though Rudolf Steiner suggested we be more universal in our thoughts when working with children, I haven't found this to be true with Lara. I am specific in my thoughts about her life and contributions, and at this point I actually sense Lara both as my daughter and as a spiritual colleague. I do feel that she is part of me, and I definitely feel like I am observing her, yet at times I can sense her observing me—in fact, I can sense this right now.

Adults have spent their appropriate time on Earth and are naturally attracted to the spiritual world. Rudolf Steiner states that when we feel sad about the loss of our adult loved ones, we do so from an egotistical standpoint. However, he also supports us in being strong enough to feel our pain. Because adults who have died have an appropriate pull toward the spiritual world, it is easier for them to approach us and contact us. It is an interesting dynamic that can feel contradictory. With adults, we want to feel as though they are observing us, because they are. And with children who have died, we feel directed to observe them.

Suicides

If your loved one had a pre-earthly intention to meet certain life challenges and have specific learning experiences and then prematurely ended their life through suicide, this will be an extremely painful experience, and they will greatly benefit from your being open to communication from them. Reading spiritual materials to them will be especially important—like applying a soothing salve to a wound—so you will want to "listen" for any cues to what they want to read. (For more on this topic, turn to chapter 10, page 155.)

Accidental Deaths

While I have had no direct experience with this situation, I would like to bring another author to your attention because of the unique story she tells. In her book *To Cause a Death: The Aftermath of an Accidental Killing*, Kelly Connor writes about her relationship with an elderly man she accidentally killed when she was seventeen years old and her personal story of healing.[5] Her work is filled with courage and can serve as a model for healing a different kind of relationship with a loved one who has died.

Veil Work Activities

Even though serving and collaborating with loved ones have been going on since the beginning of time, in this era we are cultivating a new behavior of being conscious of this communication. I encourage you to investigate the unique ways you give and receive messages. Your Daily Review will support you in this.

Activity 1: Your Daily Review Practice

Your Daily Review is a simple practice but a powerful one. For this activity, you can keep a separate notebook or journal in your nightstand drawer and write in it every evening. You can use the same journal to document what you are aware of as you wake in the morning (see activity 2).

Before you go to sleep at night, look back over your day, reviewing what happened from the end of it all the way to the start of your morning. As you do your review, think about and feel into:

- Any encounters you had—or didn't have but were scheduled to have. Note any feelings or thoughts that came to you while you were in conversation with this person, or what else came your way if the encounter did not happen.
- Thoughts that came to you. Note any that are unusual, that seemed out of the blue, or that were persistent.
- Actions that you felt compelled to do or not do.
- Feelings that came up for you that might seem out of the ordinary, or any feeling that accompanied you throughout your day.

Do not add any judgments about what you observe; record your observations just as they happened at the time. And a gentle reminder: date your entry. I recommend that you write the above instructions on one of the first pages of the main veil work journal you created in chapter 4, for easy reference.

Activity 2: Morning Awareness

In the same journal, write down what comes toward you in those magic moments just as you awaken; be open to receiving images, sounds, messages, or fragrances.

Activity 3: Observations

For at least five minutes:

- Bring into your mind your own child or another child you know who has died. Practice observing them. Can you create this observation from a feeling perspective?

- Practice being observed by your adult loved one in the spiritual world. Can you build this observation by re-creating common thoughts and memories that you and your loved one share?

Record any observations. Can you articulate the difference between how it feels to observe a child and how it feels to be observed by an adult?

Activity 4: Discerning the Quality of Messages
I introduced this chapter with two quotes. Now I invite you to return to them and read them again. Briefly describe in your journal how Rudolf Steiner's and Stuart Wilde's words impacted you. Can you identify three qualities of genuine guidance you received?

Further Reading

Staying Connected: How to Continue Your Relationships with Those Who Have Died by Rudolf Steiner, Anthroposophic Press, 1999.
To Cause a Death: The Aftermath of an Accidental Killing by Kelly Connor, Clairview, 2004.

Part 4

Reading Spirit-Filled Works

Now we are moving into the heart of veil work: your reading practice. Not only is reading spirit-filled works aloud a relatively easy way for you to reach across the veil, but it is also one of the most supportive, meaningful things you can do to serve your deceased loved ones. The first chapter in this part explores why this practice is so important, and the following two chapters will help you decide exactly what would be good choices to read, including recommendations for specific books I have found invaluable in my own reading practice.

9

Why Reading Spiritual Materials Is The Heart of Our Practice

To read to the dead is of untold significance.
—Rudolf Steiner[1]

For most of us, the love we share with our family and friends is essential to living a fulfilling life in the physical world. To live an *extraordinary* life, we can add the pursuit of knowledge and wisdom through a commitment to lifelong learning and meaningful experiences. A purposeful quest for wisdom not only enhances the richness of our own lives, but it increases our capacity to give to others—those closest to us, our communities, our professions, and the world as a whole.

In terms of *what* knowledge we pursue while we are alive, our choices are virtually limitless. We can learn about the material world or the spiritual world—or both. But it is important to understand that when we die, *only our understanding of the spiritual essence of material creations and of the spiritual world itself will go with us over the threshold.* Yes, to be fully functioning humans on Earth, we need to take interest in and explore the physical world around us. But after we die our knowledge of the purely material will be left behind; it is nonessential information in the spiritual world.

The Need for Spiritual Knowledge Beyond the Threshold

We will talk more about the experiences of our loved ones who have died in chapters 17 and 18 on the soul's journey, but for purposes of talking about our reading practice, it is important to recognize that when a person dies they enter the spiritual world with *only* the spiritual knowledge they gained from their most recent incarnation and the collective spiritual knowledge they cultivated in preceding cycles of birth and death. In other words, the fact that we have entered the spiritual world does not mean we are automatically enlightened.

What if our loved one pursued spiritual knowledge during their last lifetime here on Earth when we knew them? Is the practice of reading spiritual materials to them still valuable? Yes, most definitely. Some people avoid spirituality altogether during their lives on Earth, while others make it a lifelong pursuit. Most people probably fall somewhere in between. Where our loved ones fall along this spectrum does not matter in veil work practice. They will always receive the spiritual benefit of our reading, whether the spiritual knowledge or content we read is new to them or not. If it is not new to them, it adds to the "will forces" that are available for their use, expanding their capacity to be active contributors in the spiritual world. Incidentally, you will find the term "will forces," a concept from Steiner's work, elsewhere in the book. You can think of will forces as the energy that it takes to complete a task. Our loved ones receive extra energy when we read to them, with which they can complete spiritual tasks or participate in spiritual activities on both sides of the veil. And considering that our spiritual task is to become

---

After we die our knowledge of the purely material will be left behind; it is nonessential information.

---

the Tenth Spiritual Hierarchy—Spirit-Man, the fully individuated spirit—it's safe to say that we can keep reading. Know, too, that the effects of our reading overflow to other beings in the spiritual world who do not have the opportunity to incarnate on Earth.

No matter what level of spiritual knowledge we have under our belt when we die, most of us will at some point experience a disorientation of sorts in the spiritual realms. For seventy-odd years (or however long we live on this Earth plane) we have grown accustomed to maneuvering around the physical world using a physical body. After we die we literally lose the ground beneath our feet. We no longer have the constructs of time and space to provide landmarks in our environment, and that means we have difficulty getting our bearings.

Let me offer an analogy that speaks to why your reading practice, especially as it concerns works that explore the spiritual realms, is also beneficial to *you*. When you are traveling to a city you have never been to before, you might enjoy the spontaneity of just meeting whatever experience comes across your path. But most people will benefit from doing at least a little bit of research to know how to navigate the city safely and to identify points of interest and experiences they want to enjoy during their time there. Rather than confining your experience, planning for the trip ahead of time offers a particular kind of freedom compared to winging it once you get there. In the same way, learning about the spiritual realms now, before you journey across the veil, will open new possibilities on the other side.

Learning While We Can

One of the gifts we have been given by God—and one that is to be found only on Earth—is freedom. Only here do we have the capacity to consciously choose to acquire knowledge and wisdom about the spiritual world, because only on Earth do we have the capacity to learn *consciously* through the powers of our ego and thinking capacities. In the spiritual world, by contrast, we navigate under the direction of spiritual beings who guide us with promptings, which we feel in the form of acknowledgement of our behavior as either good or bad.

As parents, we guide and direct our children—we don't give them full-on explanations of all the whys and wherefores that underlie our advice. In fact, we don't actually need to give detailed explanations: a child knows how to discern between a parent's joyful expression and a "Don't do that," warning look. Similarly, in the spiritual world, spiritual beings within the hierarchies there watch and guide us. We *feel* promptings that guide us to this or that behavior. Through your work at the veil, you can begin to cultivate what this feels like. But as this concerns your reading practice, you consciously delve into spiritual knowledge in service to your loved ones in veil work because *this is the time when you can.* Here and now, you have the ability to offer what you learn to your loved ones inhabiting the spiritual world, where the avenue of deliberate, systematic acquisition of spiritual knowledge is closed. If in the spiritual world your loved ones recognize that they could have learned more spiritually while on Earth, they will experience remorse. Through your reading practice, you can help alleviate this.

Your Loved Ones Want to Reconnect

Here on Earth, if you move to a different part of the country or world, distant from those you love, you wouldn't think of losing

---

*Only on Earth do we have the capacity
to choose to acquire knowledge and wisdom
about the spiritual world.*

---

touch with them. Especially now, with the Internet and communication tools like Skype, maintaining contact is easy. You might choose to stay actively in touch, or your connection might dwindle and lie dormant for a time as you and those you care about live your busy lives. But you wouldn't think of cutting them off, letting go of them completely, because you know this would be hurtful to both your loved one and yourself. Well, the same is true for your loved ones who have died. They have a vested interest in your well-being and in the well-being of earthly evolution. They are longing to reach you, and for you to reach out to them. *Your reading practice is the fundamental conduit for that connection.*

In past civilizations and in tribal cultures, people celebrate death as a birth into the spiritual world, and remain connected to their ancestors. But as a result of our generally overzealous love of materials things and the material world, for most of us in modern cultures today, maintaining a connection with the spiritual world is a much harder task. We feel separated from the spiritual world, whether we are conscious of the separation or not, and as a result we feel a perception of death that is frightening instead of something to be celebrated. Today our whole society supports a mind-set that when a person we love dies, our job is to "let them go" in an appropriate amount of time—as defined by society, not by us. And we are to let them go so that they can do "their thing" in the spiritual world, as if what they do in the spiritual world is disconnected from and has nothing to do with humanity. But those who are in the spiritual world know their intimate connection with us in the physical world. It is we who are disconnected from the other side of the veil. Many of us still don't get that we are to work hand in hand with our loved ones and other spiritual beings to further the spiritual evolution of all. It is important to know that your loved ones across the veil are not constrained by that mind-set. They are looking for you, and they don't want you to break the connection. In fact, your loved ones feel pain when they cannot find you and they feel that the connection is lost.

I am not advocating that you do veil work out of a sense of guilt or obligation, because you feel you "should" address this type of pain: that's not helpful for anyone's spiritual evolution. Rather, I am suggesting that we all take this information into account and freely decide whether to engage in the selfless service of reaching across the veil. And if you decide to commit to this "deed of purest love," I am suggesting that you freely decide how much time and energy you are willing to invest in maintaining a connection that, you now know, does not need to be severed at death. Let me offer a thought that another person who has made a conscious practice of reading to the dead shared with me: "It seems to me *it is hard for the dead when everyone dismisses them as dead*."

I will close this chapter with a few more insights I have gained over the years about this core practice of reading spirit-filled works:

- When you and your loved ones both want to foster connection and their spiritual eyes are directed to the Earth, you want them to be able to find you. Reading spiritual materials to them makes this easier because you "light up" when you are filled with spiritual thoughts and feelings. Then they can "read" you, just as you can read a physical book.
- Reading spiritual materials to your loved ones gives them a form of spiritual nourishment that supports and sustains them on their spiritual journey. You need the right fuel to keep your body functioning well in the physical world. Similarly, those in the spiritual world need appropriate nourishment.

- It is very possible that your loved ones didn't have an opportunity to cultivate spiritual thoughts, feelings, and experiences while they were living in the physical world. It's possible that they didn't understand the importance of doing so, or that their life circumstance didn't support it. Your reading helps address the lack of access to this knowledge when they were alive.
- Depending on the reading material you choose (the subject of the next two chapters), you may be able to provide an orientation to what your loved one is encountering in the spiritual world. You can be their personal "travel guide" to life beyond the veil.
- Your reading will increase your loved one's capacity to contribute to *both* the spiritual and physical worlds in a positive way by providing spiritual information that will support them in their future incarnations.
- Reading practice benefits you and others here in the physical world when your loved ones take the spiritual thoughts and feelings you offer, further them in the spiritual world, and then return them to you or someone else in the form of a "new and improved" inspiration.
- Reading practice also provides the foundation for doing co-creative work across the veil. I find this area of collaboration very exciting, with immense potential for increasing good works in the world of the living.
- Your reading practice is a key element of spiritual leadership. By expanding your current spiritual practices to include practices that involve the dead, you are researching today the spiritual practices that will be commonplace in the future.

Finally, through your reading practice, you will create a sweet, grace-filled intimacy between you and your loved ones. Need I say more?

Veil Work Activities: Contemplations

How would you describe your level of knowledge of the spiritual world? What is the level of your desire to know more about it? Dig deep—do you have any discomfort about studying the spiritual world? Or does the thought of wanting to understand more about it resonate completely with you? Both are appropriate feelings and thoughts and, not uncommonly, we can hold them simultaneously.

In the spiritual world, we feel watched over and guided to appropriate action by the spiritual beings of the higher hierarchies. Practice feeling that you are being watched by a spiritual being. This could be your guiding angel, an archangel like Michael, or any other spiritual being you are familiar with. What does it feel like to know that this being is watching over your every thought, feeling, and action?

In this chapter I gave you several reasons why reading is the foundation of this work. Please review and ponder them once again. Allow your heart to inform your mind. What is the primary reason for *your* reading practice?

Enjoy journaling your findings.

10

Choosing Spiritual Materials To Read

Imagine a soul living here in the physical body who, between awaking and going to sleep, is concerned only with thoughts taken from the material world. Such a soul—filled entirely with thoughts, concepts, ideas, and sensations taken solely from the material world—cannot be perceived at all from the other world. Not one trace of it can be seen. But a soul filled with spiritual ideas … a soul glowing and illuminated by spiritual ideas is perceptible from the other world. Consequently, no matter how good they may be as human beings, the souls left behind who are immersed in materialism are not real to the world beyond and cannot be perceived.
—Rudolf Steiner[1]

In the last chapter you learned that reading materials of a spiritual nature is the foundation of veil work, the most important action you can take to serve your loved ones in the spiritual world. This leads to a question: what should you choose to read to them? You might be thinking, *Hmmm, I am not sure where to even begin this step.* Or you might be at the other end of the spectrum: *Oh my goodness, I have so many book titles swimming in my head right now, I don't know which one to start with.* Maybe you are somewhere in between. In this chapter I would like to share several different ways you can go about choosing.

Start by Asking Your Loved One

This may seem like an obvious place to start, but it's an easy one to miss. Take out your journal, enter the date, and write down the question: [Loved One], what do you want me to read to you? Or, as you will soon see, your question can actually take the form of a statement from your loved one to you.

Suppose you are thinking about what to read to your deceased father. If you are new to veil work, you may find it helpful to go back to the page in your journal that you have dedicated to your father and review some of the sensory prompts you listed that support your image of him. Bring into your mind and heart anything you have written about the contributions he made to your life and to the lives of others. That is the first step.

The next step is something you can do at any time of the day, but my favorite times are in the morning when I am doing my regular reading practice and right before I go to bed at night. Bring your father to mind—as vividly as you can, using whatever helps bring his image to life. Now put yourself in the image with him. See yourself and your father sitting or standing together, side by side.

Ask your father what he would like you to read, or see him telling you what he wants to read. To do the latter, picture him making a statement: "[Your name], here is the book (or poem, lecture, or other written material) I would like you to read to me." Picture your father holding up a book with the front cover facing toward you, and watch and listen as he speaks the title of the book out loud. Picture him lit up with joy, with a big smile of delight at the thought of you reading this book to him.

Now see yourself in the image you are holding of the two of you together. Picture the moment when you understand what the title of the book is. Your emotional expression in this scene might be delight too, or enthusiasm: "Got it!"

You can even take the vision a step further and see the two of you sitting down at a table and you reading the book to him.

This method may or may not work for you right away, but I think it is the best place to start. If it does not work the first time, you might return to it after you have more experience with veil work, and try again.

You may also find that after you try this, a book shows up in your life via another person, or on your next trip to the bookstore or library—the very book you could see your father holding up for you to see.

Your Loved One's Favorites

If you don't get a response when you ask your loved one, it makes sense to start with the spiritual materials that were their favorites. These could be books, prayers, or meditations. They could be from the spiritual stream or tradition your loved one grew up with, that they converted to as an adult, or that they simply showed an interest in or had a passion for.

If I want to choose a reading that honors my mother—on Mother's Day or the anniversary of her birth or death date, if my intention is to connect with her in a special way, or if I simply have a question just for her—I will choose a passage she marked in her personal Bible, which I now have. Not only is the spiritual essence of the passages deeply connected to her, but running my fingers over the same pages that hers touched connects us even more fully. I love knowing the passages that were important to her. I can also use any of them as my opening prayer for her.

If your loved one was a Hindu, your first selection might be from

---

If you don't get a response when you ask your loved one what to read, it makes sense to start with the spiritual books or materials that were their favorites.

---

the *Bhagavad Gita*. If they were Sufi, you could choose instead the poetry of Rumi or Hafiz. If they showed no interest in a spiritual tradition but you know they loved being in nature, something by Wendell Barry or Gary Snyder, or the poetry of Mary Oliver, might be appropriate.

Consider When You Met

Another clue to follow when you are deciding what to read is to consider where you were on your spiritual path when you first met your loved one, and how that path changed over the years when you knew each other. Our destiny and karma bring certain people into our lives for specific reasons, and at the foundation of your relationship you might find the spiritual challenges and opportunities that brought the two of you together.

What was going on in your outer and inner worlds at the time of your meeting? If you can remember, pay particular attention to what your inner world looked like at that time. Did you meet your loved one during a time in your life when you were interested in a certain spiritual stream or area of study? Maybe your loved one was mildly interested, or even showed no interest at all, but that spiritual stream was alive for you at the time. It would be exciting spiritual research to see their response if you revisit that time period with them by choosing a spiritual book that you were reading then.

If the first three options I have suggested provide no ideas, that is not a problem. Remember: this work is highly individual, and trial and error is a part of it. It just means that it is time for you to step up and take spiritual leadership in making a selection on your own. Here are some ideas that may guide you in your selection process.

Select Works from Your Own Spiritual Path

This may be the easiest answer to the question of what to read. Jump in with a book that reflects your current spiritual path, the one you find most inspiring right now. Anything at all that appeals to you will work fine, as long as it reflects spiritual truths and you are moved by the material.

Choose a Prayer or Poem

Prayers and spiritual verses are like exquisite pearls; there is great depth packed into a small number of words. Even though I have collected quite a few prayers and poems through the years, I generally use only two to five during a reading session. These writings are particularly effective in increasing your readiness for veil work. When you choose just the right one, your heart is warmed and your soul is prepared for the devotion and purity of love that are necessary for this work. It is a good sign if you can physically feel genuine warmth throughout your heart area and chest: that warmth will then permeate your entire being.

Prayers and spiritual verses are like exquisite pearls; there is great depth packed into a small number of words.

While I might read from a book for the majority of my reading time, I like to at least start and end my session with a prayer or poem. Again, if you are aware that your loved one had favorites, you can start there, but if they never shared any favorites with you, choose your own.

If you have no favorites yourself, now is the time to start exploring! Pick up the works of Jalal ad-Din Muhammad Rumi, Rainer Maria Rilke, Rabindranath Tagore, Kahlil Gibran, Ralph Waldo Emerson, Rudolf Steiner, or Antonio Machado to start. Or ask family or friends if they have any favorite poets or prayers.

You can even create your own prayer using the basic structure of one that you are familiar with, as I did when I wrote "Lynn's Prayer" taking after the Lord's Prayer:

Lynn's Prayer

Lynn,
you who were, are, and will be
in your inmost being.

May you glorify and praise
the Divine within.

May your kingdom grow
in your deeds and
may you softly touch others' lives.

May you perform your will
as you know it to be true
in your inmost being.

You have a spiritual reservoir
so abundant
that it will sustain you
in all the changing conditions
of your life.

Let your compassion toward others
make up for the sins
done to your being.

You do not allow the tempter
to work in you.

For no temptation can live
in your being,
Lynn,
for the tempter is only appearance
and delusion,
which is illuminated by the
light of your knowledge.

May you honor your power
and use it for glorious work
through all periods
and ages
of time.
Amen.

—Lynn Rollins Stull

If you don't have a prayer you want to follow and personalize, start with a blank sheet of paper and write what you heart longs to say.

Where Are They and What Are They Doing?

If you are like me, you long to understand where exactly your loved one is in the spiritual world and the many possible adventures they might be experiencing. If that is the case, I can highly recommend you read any one of Rudolf Steiner's collections of lectures on what happens after we die and what the spiritual worlds are like. One of the first books I read on this subject was *Life Beyond Death*.[2] If you align spiritually with the Buddhist tradition, you might read instead from the pages of the *Tibetan Book of the Dead*.

Did Your Loved One Have an Unfulfilled Dream or Passion?

My mother was, for the most part, a self-trained artist. However, I can remember only a few occasions as a child and teenager when I actually saw her at her easel, painting. It seems that her painting supplies were always neatly stowed out of sight when the family was home.

At one point in my mother's life, she stopped painting altogether. When I visited Mother and Dad as an adult, I missed seeing any new works of my mother's around the house. Mother was a better than average artist who displayed her artistic abilities in how she cared for our home and in the part-time job she took as an interior decorator. I don't know for sure if she had an unfilled dream of sharing her artistry with the world. If she didn't—me being an admirer of hers—I would have loved to have seen that happen. But regardless, because of my mother's clear interest in color, I feel confident in saying that she was the one who inspired me to choose many of the books on my shelf about the spiritual qualities of colors, including books about and a study of the technique of Liane Collot d'Herbois, in particular *Light, Darkness and Colour in Painting Therapy.*[3]

If something like this sounds true of your loved one—that they had a passion they were not able to fulfill when you knew them—I highly suggest reading about how that interest can be spiritualized. This may alleviate any discomfort they may be experiencing, any "residue" of a longing they had on Earth that may not have been completely satisfied. It will also prepare them to explore this area in their next incarnation.

Follow Your Spiritual Interests

> Better two than one by himself, since thus their work is really profitable. (Ecclesiastes 4:9[4])

Do you have unanswered spiritual questions? Would you like to engage your loved one in helping you answer them? Read a book on a spiritual topic you want to gain wisdom about. Picture your loved one on the other side of the veil taking those concepts and then, either by themselves or with the help of higher spiritual beings, developing them further and returning them back to you. This beautiful give and take of ideas and the intentional development of spiritual wisdom are true wonders at the veil.

More Areas to Explore

Spiritual Hierarchies

I mentioned in chapter 9 that our spiritual task as humans is to become the Tenth Spiritual Hierarchy—Spirit-Man. Nine spiritual hierarchies exist that are higher than we are. In ascending order, they are: angels, archangels, archai, exusiai, dynamis, kyriotetes, thrones, cherubim, and seraphim. All of these spiritual beings depend on our spiritual growth and are ripe for exploration through reading. What essential contribution to spiritual evolution does a type of spiritual being make? How do you engage your angel? I have learned that like most of our loved ones who have died, most angels are underutilized and are waiting for us to enlist their help.

Many of the resources I have consulted about angels are vague in their descriptions of the duties and responsibilities these beings carry, so there is much to learn in this area. Think about it: if you were to describe each member of your family to a friend, you would not be vague. Each family member has unique qualities you could easily name. The same is true with the spiritual hierarchies; each one has a primary quality and task that it is responsible for. The deeper our understanding of these, the more opportunity we have to deepen our relationship to them and to understand how we serve one another and how we can support our loved ones who have died. Additionally, I think that understanding the qualities and tasks of the spiritual hierarchies will help us discern whether it is our angels or our loved ones who are contacting us.

I can recommend three titles for this area of study, all compilations of lectures by Rudolf Steiner: *Angels*, a study of our connection with our individual angel and the tasks of the lowest rank;[5] *Spiritual Beings in the Heavenly Bodies and in the Kingdoms of Nature*, which teaches how to recognize and come to know the activities and beings of the nine angelic hierarchies;[6] and *The Spiritual Hierarchies and the Physical World: Zodiac, Planets & Cosmos*, which takes a more cosmic view of the hierarchies.[7] This last book is a little more difficult to penetrate so I would recommend it for the serious student.

For an example of how this can be helpful, I have learned that if I want to delve deeper into the mysteries of speech and eurythmy, even though other hierarchies are involved in our capacity to speak, one of them is directly related to movement: dynamis. This, then, is the spiritual hierarchy I would want to better understand and add to my reading practice.

Spiritual Festivals and Events

Do you celebrate any traditional spiritual festivals? Do you know the spiritual impulses that lie beneath the major spiritual celebrations of the world, especially those that are not from your own spiritual tradition? How can you invite your loved one to be part of the festivities?

An excellent choice for a reading topic would be to make the study of spiritual festivals a yearlong activity, creating a calendar that highlights all of the major religions and spiritual streams. You could work on identifying the common threads as well as articulating the unique differences, and investigate the path of spiritual evolution that comes from each of them. Volumes have been written about all of the major spiritual festivals: the Hindu Diwali, the Christian Epiphany, the Muslim Ramadan, and countless others. These would all be fruitful topics to explore with your loved one.

Karma and Reincarnation

You read about this topic in chapter 2, and there are many intriguing books you could read to explore it. In addition to the ones I listed on page 33, you might investigate *Many Mansions* by Gina Cerminara, which explores how Edgar Cayce used past life information for healing clients.[8] Another good choice is *Many Lives, Many Masters* by Brian L. Weiss.[9] Rudolf Steiner's *Karmic Relationships: Esoteric Studies*, an eight-volume lecture series on looking at the underlying laws of reincarnation and karma, is an excellent source for study.[10] One of my favorites is *Manifestations of Karma*. In this lecture series, Steiner gives examples of how our individual karma interweaves with others and larger groups of people.[11]

Compare Different Religions and Spiritual Streams

You can explore the teachings of religions worldwide, the common denominators that underlie them, and the spiritual impulses that have influenced them. When you consider past and current spiritual streams and religions, can you imagine what new ones will be birthed in the future?

Comparative religion is of course an enormous topic. Sometimes when I am looking to enter into a subject matter that seems complicated, I look for a children's book that will give me an overview. Peter Bedrick's *Young People's Encyclopedia of Religions of the World* does a nice job of dividing the contents of this subject over general areas: ancient religions, with a historical picture of where religion has evolved from; religions that have a single book as their central tenet (Judaism, Christianity, Islam); Eastern religions (Hinduism, Jainism, Sikhism, Buddhism, Confucianism, Taoism, Shinto), and traditional beliefs (African religions, religions of Oceania, and religions of the Native Americans). This will no doubt generate many ideas for further study.[12]

Possible New Spiritual Impulses

Is spirituality coded into our DNA? I would like to mention two books in this area: Lynda Bunnell and Ra Uru Hu's *The Definitive Book of Human Design*[13] and Richard Rudd's *Gene Keys*.[14] Both books use your birth chart to analyze your genetically given spiritual traits with the understanding that by knowing your own spiritual genetic design, you will be better able to step into your more spiritual, higher self. On a personal note, I worked up human design charts for Lara and myself and am in the process of doing a comparative study of where our spiritual traits intersect and complement each other. This is proving to be a fascinating study!

Spiritual Leaders and Leadership

Here is another exciting area to explore that has endless qualified subjects. You can choose from books by or about global leaders who, through their spiritual faith and discipline, created social reforms, brought about new spiritual impulses, or demonstrated how to spiritualize practical activities. Of course, the one who inspires me most is Rudolf Steiner, but here are several other spiritual leaders to consider:

Mohandas Gandhi (1869–1948). A lawyer by profession, Gandhi led a nonviolent movement for civil rights in South Africa and independence in India. While he was a student of all religions, he was a devoted Hindu.

The Fourteenth Dalai Lama, born Lhamo Thondup (1935–), Tibet's political and spiritual leader who was determined at the age of two to be the successor to the Thirteenth Dalai Lama. All Dalai Lamas are regarded as the incarnation of a significant Buddhist deity and the embodiment of compassion.

Martin Luther King, Jr. (1929–1968), a Baptist minister, orator, leader, and role model for nonviolent civil disobedience based on his Christian beliefs who advanced civil rights for African Americans.

Dr. Sakena Yacoobi is the founder of the Afghan Institute of Learning and recipient of five honorary doctorates. Her work, which is focused on education and health care, has been credited with helping more than 12 million people. She told *The Huffington Post,* "I really believe that Islam says that education is a must for both men and women. The Quran tells us to be good, and education gives you critical thinking skills that are essential for ethical decision-making." Her website is afghaninstituteoflearning.org.[15]

Wilma Mankiller (1945–2010) was one of the few women to lead a major Native American tribe, the Cherokee Nation. She focused her work exclusively on social programs and later became a teacher.

She received the highest civilian award in the United States, the Presidential Medal of Freedom, in 1998.

The Pope (currently Francis) is the leader of the Catholic Church and successor to Saint Peter, the one about whom Jesus said, "You are Peter and on this rock I will build my Church." (Matthew 16:18)

Joan of Arc (1412–1431), the patron saint of France, received spiritual visions to lead the French army against the British invaders during the Hundred Years' War. Joan was known for her piety, chastity, and humility.

Hildegard of Bingen (1098–1179), was a mystic, composer, and author of books on spirituality, health and nutrition, and nature. Through meditation she nurtured an intimate relationship with God and received visions. She was influential among many leaders, both religious and secular.

Mani (216–274), of Iranian origin, was a prophet and the founder of Manichaeism, which taught that the world was both spirit and matter and the scene of constant struggle between light and darkness, good and evil.

Socrates (~470–399 BCE), a Greek thinker. Plato, a major founder of Western philosophy, was one of his students. Justice and striving toward Goodness were themes that wove through his teachings.

Meister Eckhart (1260–1327), a German mystic and theologian whose philosophy was to see God in all people and everything.

Kasper (or Casper) Hauser (~1812–1831), held captive until fifteen or sixteen years of age when he appeared in the streets of Nuremberg, Germany, barely able to walk and unable to speak. A mystery surrounds the possibility that he was born a prince and would have contributed to the spiritual unfolding of humanity if he had not died young.

Pema Chödrön (1936–), an American nun in the Tibetan Buddhist tradition, mother and grandmother, author, and speaker. "If one wishes suffering not to happen to the people and the earth, it begins with a kind heart."[16]

Ralph Waldo Emerson (1803–1882) was a philosopher and writer who led the Transcendentalist movement in the mid-nineteenth century in response to the rise of intellectualism and spirituality. This movement believed in the good of human beings, who could act from their own inner knowing versus looking outside of themselves. Emerson wrote essays and poems and was a lecturer. He has influenced many writers, poets, and philosophical thinkers, from his time through the present.

Thich Nhat Hanh (1926–) coined the term "engaged Buddhism." He is a Vietnamese Buddhist monk, teacher, and author of more than a hundred books. He is also a renowned peace activist.

Nelson Mandela (1918–2013), former president of South Africa, anti-apartheid revolutionary, and statesman. He also worked to alleviate poverty and eliminate HIV/AIDS. His spiritual influences included his Methodist upbringing, Ghandhi's model of nonviolence, and the African principle of *Ubuntu:* kindness to others.

Malala Yousafzai (1997–) is a Pakistani activist for education, especially for females. She is a co-winner of the 2014 Nobel Peace Prize. She has campaigned and even risked her life to fulfill the Quran's words: "Seeking knowledge is obligatory upon every Muslim." In her autobiography, Malala writes, "Education is our right. Just as it is our right to sing. Islam has given us this right and says that every girl and boy should go to school."[17]

One of my favorite discoveries was a compilation of lectures by Ehrenfried Pfeiffer in a beautiful little book entitled *Spiritual Leadership of Mankind*. Pfeiffer discusses Saint Francis's spiritual leadership, including his connection to both the Buddha and the Christ. Francis's exemplary life reflected twelve specific virtues that were also embodied by each of the order's twelve original friars: "faith, simplicity, courtesy, gracious and natural sense, the mind raised in contemplation, virtuous and continual labor, patience, the Imitation of Christ, charity, solicitude [care or concern for others], humility, fairness."[18]

Pfeiffer suggests that knowledge of these virtues will support us in the time period shortly after we die. We will talk more about this in the section on the soul's journey after death, but briefly, after we die there is a time when we review how we have treated others. It is during this time that a deep understanding of Saint Francis's virtues can provide spiritual fortitude and reduce the time we spend in review, allowing us to advance more quickly to the higher regions of the spiritual world. Our loved ones in this area of the spiritual world may also receive benefits through our comprehending of what made Saint Francis a spiritual leader.

Readings for Special Circumstances

If You Are Reading to Your Child

> A "child" can be a highly evolved individual, able to guide one to things (in the spiritual world) that can otherwise be discovered only with great difficulty. Consequently, I would say that, yes, one also can practice reading to children who die young.[19]

Most of the time I still hold an image of Lara as she was when she was alive. In recent years, though, I vacillate between seeing her as a child and as I think she might be as a young woman and my spiritual colleague. I have always felt that my daughter was much more spiritually advanced than I am, so I never experienced an inner question about whether it was appropriate to read her "adult" spiritual materials. Because I was interested in what experiences the spiritual world held for my daughter, I dove into Rudolf Steiner's *Life Between Death and Rebirth,* a book of lectures.[20] By following my initial interest, I seemed to be "led" to the next book, and then to subsequent books. My experience has taught me that you can read to children as though they were adults, even if the main image you hold of your loved one is of a small child.

Selections for Those Who Have Taken Their Own Lives

One morning very early on in my reading practice, a woman I had worked with about eight years prior to Lara's death, and who had committed suicide about a year and a half after I met her, seemed to "appear" at my regular reading time. When I say "appear," I mean I saw her name, Doreen, and an image of her as I last remembered her. I received a feeling from her that can best be described as an urgent longing to be included in my readings. Her addition to my group of regulars reminded me of several other people who had also committed suicide: one of my mother's friends, Dorothy, and the sister of a high school friend, Suzette. I brought to mind both Dorothy and Suzette on several occasions, but I was not able to perceive direct feedback from either of them.

Very often those who have taken their own lives will feel quite disoriented in the spiritual world. A book that I have found very helpful in understanding how to work with a loved one who has committed suicide is Dore Deverell's *Light Beyond The Darkness.*[21] Deverell's thirty-six-year-old son committed suicide, and the book is about what led up to that act, as well as her connection with and continuing service to her son after he reincarnated. She relates the experience of meeting a child who—although she wanted to dismiss the promptings in the beginning—she recognized was her deceased child reincarnated. I spoke once with Ms. Deverell on the phone and found her very down to earth and matter of fact about her work with her son. It was satisfying to speak with another mother who saw this work of being of service to our loved ones as of the utmost importance. Ms. Deverell died on July 2, 2013, at age ninety.

By now it will be clear that your choice of spiritual materials to read is virtually limitless. Yet there is still more to consider! In the next chapter, we will shift the discussion to readings that help to spiritualize common activities—lifting the everyday to a higher purpose.

Veil Work Activities

In addition to the activities that follow here, be sure to explore the Eight-Step Process for Creating a Spiritual Reading Practice at the end of the next chapter.

- Quiet yourself. Connect with God and your angel. Remind yourself of your intention for this work with your loved one. Is your intention to provide spiritual nourishment or to give them an orientation to where they are in the spiritual realms? Or could your loved one benefit from gaining a spiritual understanding about a particular topic? What is the best way you can serve your loved one? I recommend that you address these questions directly to God. Write down in your journal the inner promptings that come forth, and engage your angel as your witness and helper in completing any required action.

- If you want to penetrate a spiritual thought, you want to look at the thought from as many perspectives and viewpoints as possible. Once you have chosen a topic and the first book or other written material to read to your loved one, is there another author who could deepen your understanding of that topic? If so, write the title of their book in your journal, and as you are reading the first book you chose, periodically check in and see if you feel a pull to read pages from the second book. Note your research in your journal.

- If you have chosen to study a biography and/or the work of a spiritual leader, here are some questions you might ponder: Did this person obtain spiritual knowledge or wisdom about the spiritual world and beings only for themselves? Or did they do so to help others, to contribute to humanity as a whole? When they brought their spiritual findings to the world, how were they able to tame their own personal ambitions and desires? Write down your thoughts and feelings in your journal.

- Do a comparison of spiritual leaders and what they stand for. Challenge yourself to draw a historical timeline, noting when spiritual impulses came through these leaders into the world, and how the impulses affected our physical world and spiritual evolution.

11

Reading To Spiritualize Common Activities

Spiritualizing the stuff of everyday living offers a forward-thinking opportunity, whether for your loved one's next incarnation or your co-creative work together in today's world. By "spiritualizing common activities," I mean taking the material deeds of life here on Earth and seeking their spiritual Truth and essence. In so doing we embody these activities with the virtue of Beauty and enliven them by practicing the art of Goodness, for today and the future.

The Arts

One fruitful activity to explore is one that humans have pursued through the ages: the general field of the arts. What spiritualizes art? Wassily Kandinsky (1866–1944) explored this topic in his classic book *Concerning the Spiritual in Art*.[1] In her review of the book, the writer and critic Maria Popova called it "an exploration of the deepest and most authentic motives for making art, the 'internal

---

By "spiritualizing common activities," I mean taking the material deeds of life here on Earth and seeking their spiritual Truth and essence.

---

necessity' that impels artists to create as a spiritual impulse and audiences to admire art as a spiritual hunger."[2]

In addition to the virtues of Truth and Goodness, I recognize the virtue of Beauty as a key element in spiritualizing art. John O'Donohue's book *Divine Beauty: The Invisible Embrace* is an excellent exploration of all the possible elements of Beauty. With poetry and poetic imagery throughout, the book is itself a work of Beauty.[3]

If you are one who feels music all the way into your bones, there is a good reason: music is the most spiritual of all the arts. Read *Spiritual Lives of the Great Composers* by Patrick Kavanaugh with the intention of seeing the essence of each composer Kavanaugh writes about.[4] For the more ambitious reader, challenge yourself with Arman Husemann's book *Human Hearing and the Reality of Music*. Husemann "elaborates on the living physiology of hearing and making music, merging the findings of neurophysiology with anthroposophical spiritual scientific studies of the human being."[5]

If your loved one was unable to fulfill a childhood desire to become a stage actor, your book selections might include *The Path of the Actor* or *Lessons for the Professional Actor*, both by Michael Chekhov. Chekhov speaks very little about his own personal philosophy and spiritual beliefs, yet the foundation of the acting techniques he is known for internationally is his interest in the wisdom of several different spiritual streams.[6]

In *Centering in Pottery, Poetry, and the Person*, author M. C. Richards infuses concepts of spirituality in the techniques she taught as a potter and poet. Richards writes that art "is a bridge between the visible and invisible worlds."[7]

William Shakespeare still stands as a mystery to many of us. What was the spiritual impulse that lay at the root of the work of the Bard of Avon? In their book *Shakespeare's Flowering of the Spirit*, Margaret Bennel and Isabel Wyatt take a look at Shakespeare's spiritual nature and how his spiritual development shines through his plays and contributes to their long-standing appeal.[8]

For more on the virtues of Truth, Beauty, and Goodness, and art as a spiritual activity, see chapters 13 and 14.

Nature Spirits and Gardening

If your loved one enjoyed being in nature and gardening, consider Susan Raven's book *Nature Spirits*, in which she explores the unseen spirits that are specific to nature and live in the elements of earth, water, air, and fire, and how having a conscious relationship with them can help us co-create a new world for the future. It might be a perfect primer for your loved one's next incarnation, educating them on these creative spirits that often go unseen and unacknowledged. This book includes meditations and exercises.[9]

Spiritualizing the Land Through Biodynamic Agriculture

If a loved one had an interest in agriculture, you might investigate biodynamic gardening, a way of spiritualizing agriculture that Rudolf Steiner developed, and a powerful alternative to conventional farming. Today's agribusiness removes farming from its cultural context and its support of the families that practice it. As a result, we as a nation are estranged from the land—from the intimate knowledge, love, and care of it.

Rather than depleting the land and tipping it out of balance as large-scale agricultural methods typically do, Steiner's method

161

actually enlivens the soil, leaving it healthier than it was before. His 1924 lectures on the subject are available at no charge.[10] Your loved one may have died before this method was created or may not have had access to it. Reading from these lectures will give them innate knowledge when they return to Earth.

The poet and farmer Wendell Berry argues that good farming is a "cultural development and spiritual discipline." He contrasts the two opposing approaches to agriculture in his book *The Unsettling of America:* "the exploiter" and "the nurturer." "The exploiter is a specialist, an expert; the nurturer is not. The standard of the exploiter is efficiency; the standard of the nurturer is care. The exploiter's goal is money, profit; the nurturer's goal is health—his land's health, his own, his family's, his community's, his country's." The nurturer, Berry explains, thinks in terms of the overall health and longevity of the system and tends to practice holistic thought.[11]

The Starry Night

Historically the night sky was a source of guidance, but today most of us are cut off from the wisdom of the night sky. My two recommendations on this topic are not for the faint of heart: Willi Sucher's book *Cosmic Christianity and the Changing Countenance of Cosmology*[12] and *Sky Phenomena* by Norman Davidson.[13] I have found that these require serious study, but like anything that takes a certain will force, satisfaction and the cultivation of discipline come from understanding even one page. With this area of study, like the topic of comparing spiritual streams, you might find this subject more approachable if you start by getting your bearings with a children's book's orientation to the night sky and then progress to books that speak to the spirituality of the stars.

You might investigate writings and courses offered by an organization like the Institute of Noetic Sciences, founded by Edgar Mitchell, an astronaut on the Apollo 14 flight to the moon. As he was returning to Earth, he felt a sense of connection to the universe, a feeling he later described as Samadhi: "The presence of divinity became almost palpable, and I knew that life in the universe was not just an accident based on random processes.... The knowledge came to me directly."[14]

From a historical perspective, the night sky was more visible to ancient peoples than it is to us as we look up through our polluted atmosphere. It was also a means of understanding their world and their place in it. For instance, astronomy taught the Mayan people what they needed to know about the order of the universe and the gods. They believed that properly observing the passage of time was essential, and in response they created sophisticated calendars. They also believed that the gods communicated with them through the movement of planets, stars, and constellations throughout the seasons. As they studied celestial movements to understand the relationship between the sky and the Earth, the Mayans used astronomy to create their own form of astrology.[15]

Business and Entrepreneurship

How happy are the poor in spirit;
theirs is the kingdom of heaven.
Happy the gentle:
they shall have the earth for their heritage.
Happy those who mourn:
they shall be comforted.
Happy those who hunger and thirst for what is right:
they shall be satisfied.
Happy the merciful:
they shall have mercy shown them.
Happy the pure in heart:
they shall see God.
Happy the peacemakers:

they shall be called sons of God.
Happy those who are persecuted in the cause of right:
theirs is the kingdom of heaven.
—The Beatitudes, Matthew 5:1–10

How do spiritual qualities and spirituality inform the workplace? Bill Bottum (1927–2005) was a fine example. He developed a personal connection to the Beatitudes, Matthew 5:1–10, beginning at the age of twenty. These verses formed his values and informed how he led his personal life as well as how he pursued his business career. To avoid intruding on others' personal beliefs, he rewrote the Beatitudes as "Guiding Principles and Attributes" for the workplace. Bottum "believed that these concepts were universal, common threads woven through the shared fabric of the great wisdom traditions. Because they show up around the world in different epochs and cultures, he also believed them to be archetypal patterns embedded deep within the human psyche."[16]

As a business executive, Bill Bottum kept abreast of developments in modern management techniques. He concluded from his studies that several "new" management methods—including partnership, empowerment, dialogue, and employee participation—followed many of the values he drew from the Beatitudes. He applied these principles to a new set of management methods that accomplished his company's business goals while living up to his guiding principles. In doing so, he achieved extraordinary success. Bottum's friends Dorothy Lenz, George SanFacon, and Larry Spears edited a collection of his ideas and writings. It is available online.[17]

Healthy Communities

The future is going to call forth the best in all of us, especially when it comes to building healthy communities. We can describe a healthy community as one in which each member is not only accepted, but respected and inspired to contribute their unique capacities and individual excellence to the group. A healthy community is sound in all areas including culture, governance, and economics. Many books have recently been written that identify key components of a healthy, sustainable community, including *Sekem: A Sustainable Community in the Egyptian Desert*[18] and *Common Wealth For a Free, Equal, Mutual, and Sustainable Society*.[19]

Veil Work Activity: An Eight-Step Process for Creating a Spiritual Reading Practice

1. Find a quiet place and time. For me, most of the time it is at my kitchen table early in the morning. Center yourself. Bring into your heart and mind your connection with God, your loved one who has died, your angel, and your loved one's angel. I also like to bring in the Christ. I like to visualize this connection and see the presence of my loved one at my kitchen table with our angels standing behind us.

2. While lighting a candle, speak your intention to serve God and your loved one through this reading practice.

3. Open your reading session by softly reading aloud a prayer or spiritual poem or verse.

4. Softly read aloud the spiritual material you have chosen, whether more prayers, your or your loved one's favorite spiritual books, or any other suggestions in this chapter. Understand fully what the material means. Infuse it with your love, interest, and enthusiasm.

5. Read for ten minutes or up to one hour. Write down what you read in your journal and take notes on any inspirations that might have come to you during this time.

6. Close by reading your opening prayer or poem again, or reading a new selection.

7. Feel a moment of gratitude toward your loved one who has died, your angels, and God.
8. Blow out the candle. Put the material you are reading in a special place for the next time you read to your loved one.

Part 5

Co-Creating Through the Veil

When I first started to read to Lara and others who had crossed the threshold, I didn't understand the concept or possibility of co-creating with her and others. Now, years later, I have an inner knowing that not only are we being loved and supported by our loved ones, but we are co-creating with them, whether we are conscious of it or not. By co-creation, I mean that they are intentionally influencing us to create change in the world, for ourselves and for others. In this part, we will explore some of the ways this can work. In chapter 12 I will give you an overview of how co-creation takes place and what to look for. Chapter 13 is a discussion of the spiritual virtues of Truth, Beauty, and Goodness, your companions in co-creating with your loved ones. We will explore art as a spiritual activity in chapter 14. In chapter 15, Using Color, I will share some theories on the spiritual aspects of color and you will have the opportunity to start working with color yourself. Finally, chapter 16, Eurythmy: Movement That Penetrates the Veil, delves into the extraordinary form of movement Rudolf Steiner developed that has become one of the cornerstones of my own veil work practice.

12

Introduction To Co-Creation

Co-creating is a fascinating aspect of veil work—an endless source of wonder for me. As I have said before, our loved ones who have died and the beings in the spiritual hierarchies have our best interest at heart and are eager to help us travel our spiritual path here on Earth. When we connect with them and follow the impulses we sense coming from them, our lives can take surprising, meaningful, and delightful turns.

Our angels play a major part in this, particularly our guardian angel, who leads us to certain experiences. As you start to look for co-creative opportunities, I think it is valuable to try to discern whether your angel or your loved one is supporting and inspiring you. I am still trying to understand the differentiation myself, and I think our personal biographies can help illuminate this mystery, as can an intensive study of the spiritual hierarchies.

If I try to be objective about my own personal biography, I feel that much of what happened before Lara died was very much supported by the activity of my personal angel. I think my guardian angel helped me follow the pathways that were true to what I thought my life should look like. Since Lara's death, co-creating with her and other loved ones who have died has directed me to

---

*Our loved ones who have died and the beings
in the spiritual hierarchies have our best interest
at heart and are eager to help us travel
our spiritual path here on Earth.*

---

venture into areas it would never occur to me to explore on my own.

There is a dance that goes on when I am co-creating with my loved ones who have died, a kind of rhythm that feels very natural to me. I do the work of reading spiritual materials, and they respond by inspiring me with projects and experiences that expand who I am, expand our spiritual capacities, and add more Truth, Beauty, and Goodness to the world, all at the same time.

In this chapter I will give you some ways to identify co-creation when it is happening and also give you some specific steps to consciously co-create with your loved ones in the spiritual world.

How to Identify When It Is About to Happen

Rudolf Steiner has illuminated some of the types of co-creative impulses you might receive and connected them with the time frame of the death of the person who is generating them. Generally speaking, he attributes certain events and meetings of people for the purpose of enriching their lives to those who have recently died. From loved ones who have been dead for twenty to thirty years, you can expect to feel an immediate, straightforward prompting in which you can feel the will of the person who has died directing you, influencing your habits and character. Loved ones who have been deceased for thirty or more years will influence your views and ideas at a moral level, a level that considers the evolution of humanity.[1]

Interest in the Other

Certain people you meet over the course of your life will have significant impact on how your life unfolds. A stranger standing in line with you at your favorite café could mention out of the blue that they are taking a photography workshop this weekend. This brief conversation ignites a desire within you to take a photography class, which then leads you to a more serious study of photography. Next thing you know, you have changed your career and are hanging out your shingle as a professional photographer.

Or you may meet someone and feel an instant connection and want to find out more about them. There is a kind of familiarity, as though you somehow remember them. This connection can lead to a lifelong friendship or a career or a marriage. Or this person seems to have arrived in your life to connect you to someone else. If you look back over your life you can note these kinds of meetings that shifted your direction, whether they seemed significant at the time or not. This type of collaboration typically comes from your loved one who has recently died.

You Get a Feeling

Have you ever decided not to attend an event or go to a friend's party, and then at the eleventh hour get a strong feeling that you should go? Have you ever been working diligently on a project, reached an impasse, and then all of a sudden got a feeling that you knew where you could find the person or information that would help you find your way to the solution? This feeling impulse usually comes from somebody who has been dead for twenty to thirty years.

You Get an Idea

Has an idea ever popped into your head that you thought could not possibly be yours? It just flew into your beautiful brain and seemed to ask you to take a particular action. This has happened to me during a variety of circumstances. For example, I woke up one morning with these words echoing in my mind: "Sing or you will lose the capacity to sing." There was strong motivation in that statement! And yes, I did decide to sing, as you will soon learn. Another time I was driving on the freeway in L.A. when the thought "A hundred eurythmy talks to celebrate a hundred years" came to me. I followed up on this thought too. I didn't actually wind up giving a hundred talks, but I did give many. Through that one idea, I was able to bring eurythmy to new audiences who had never experienced it before, including inmates in a Southern California women's prison, a management team at a health care provider, and local church congregations. When ideas come out of the blue like this, they are typically coming from a loved one who has been dead for more than thirty years.

You Experience Extra Strength

Here is something else you may observe: finding that you have more strength or extra will forces that enable you to complete a project that you otherwise would not have the strength for. Going to eurythmy school over a period of years and then earning my diploma at the age of fifty-four is probably the best example from my life. The physical and emotional stamina it took to accomplish this was beyond my own, yet I felt as if I was graced with extra strength—and I was. When a child dies, they bring with them into the spiritual world the extra life forces that they normally would have used for living out a normal lifespan. My daughter graced me with this extra strength. It is quite humbling to ponder this concept.

Recognizing your interest in another, a feeling that urges you in a particular direction, or an inspiring idea that does not seem to be yours all require a certain level of self-knowledge. You will be developing greater self-knowledge as you continue with your veil work practice.

The Picture of Who We Co-Create with Is Changing

Yes, we co-create with loved ones to whom we are related. But today the group of people we can co-create with is expanding beyond our hereditary connections. A familial lineage is not as essential as it once was. And it is interesting to note that this expansion of co-creation opportunities is happening at a time when we can make global connections on Earth more easily than ever before. Today we are creating communities in our neighborhoods as well as through the Internet, and communities are coming together for an infinite number of reasons.

Steps That Support Conscious Co-Creation

In addition to following the steps for a successful veil work practice—committing to a regular reading practice and following the guidelines for effective communication outlined in chapters 7 and 8—conscious co-creation also requires that you further develop your openness to and awareness of communication from across the veil.

Develop Greater Awareness

Practice noticing the finer details of what is going on in your life. A co-creative message can take a variety of forms. It might be a fairly obvious tap on the shoulder, a clear message that says, "Here's what I would like you to do," as was the case for me when I received the message through a friend: "You need to write this book." Or it can be much less direct. Here are some thoughts and questions to keep in mind as you practice the skill of awareness:

- Note the finer, more intimate connections that arise between you and someone else.

---

*Practice noticing the finer details of what
is going on in your life. A co-creative message
can take a variety of forms.*

- What happens, or doesn't happen. For example, let's say you always put your keys in the same place, but this morning you can't find them and now you are late. Or there is the classic "wrong turn," where you literally turn down a wrong road and end up at a different destination than you intended. Or you see someone you haven't seen in years. Ask yourself: How did that happen? What happened, or didn't? What unexpected experience did you have that expanded your spiritual capacities, or added Goodness to the world?

- When you enter a room, what is the energy there? How does each individual in the room affect the energy of the room? Can you notice who you feel interested in?

- Who did you meet during the day? Did your conversation reveal something? I once went to a small jazz concert by myself in a dinner theater setting. I was not there to dine, but when I arrived for the show and looked around the room, I was struck by the thought of asking to sit at a table where a woman was sitting alone. She smiled and said sure, and we chatted before the concert started. During intermission, I asked her if she played a musical instrument. She said no, but told me she was a singer. That out-of-the-blue message "Sing or you will lose your capacity to sing" popped into my thoughts, and I asked her where she sang. It turned out she was in the local community choir. It wasn't currently in session, but she said she would be glad to contact me when the next session started. I gave her my phone number and that was that ... or so I thought. One afternoon I was sitting at my kitchen table working, and the phone rang. The woman on the other end of the line briskly said, "The community choir starts again this Monday evening at seven. Rehearsals are at the high school. I won't be able to attend but have fun." Then she hung up before I could even thank her or ask her if she could remind me of her name. Because of this woman I had a sudden impulse to sit with—to this day I still do not know her name—I responded to the call I received upon waking one day, and I am very happy to be sharing in the experience of singing in a lovely choir.

Acknowledge Your Co-Creative Messages

When your loved one steps forward to direct you toward a creative act, let them know you heard them. Say, "Yes! This feels like an impulse from my loved ones, and I freely take action. I commit to completing this project with them." This is an excellent time to note in your journal the date and what the co-creation will be, and also document what led up to this moment—how did the inspiration come to you? Can you discern which of your loved ones is guiding you to this experience? Is it more than one person? It doesn't take long for our loved ones to get that we are willing to work with them. In fact, they delight in our willingness to co-create with them.

Be Grateful

After you have completed the task you were given—whether it was committing to a relationship that supported you in creating something new in the world with that other person, following a feeling that led to a new educational experience, acting on an idea that you received, or putting to use the extra will forces that gave you the strength to fulfill a task—give gratitude to God, your loved one, and the angelic realm that helped you complete the task. Gratitude will warm your heart and help you culminate your work together. Allow yourself a moment to express, "Well done!"

Veil Work Activities

- Investigate your personal biography. Set aside about two to three hours and look back from the present to when you were born. Note significant life changes and experiences and see if you can match them with meeting particular people or certain events in your life. Identify what was spiritually important in that experience. Do you have a feeling about whether these significant life changes were connected to the past, were a present necessity, or were future oriented? Do you feel you were particularly inspired by your angel or a loved one?

- Do your Daily Review. Get into the routine of going through your day and making notes in your journal about people you spent time with and experiences you had. Notice people and things you were interested in, strong or subtle feelings, any random thoughts that seem significant, or times when you found you had extra strength to finish a project.

- Time for brainstorming. Journal any dreams you have for the future. Pick one that has a spiritual impulse at its center. Make a list of ideas for how your loved ones could help you co-create that dream. Then bring your dream to your loved ones, either during your reading sessions, or as you are falling asleep, and ask them for their assistance.

13

Truth, Beauty, and Goodness: Your Companions in Co-Creation

Veil work practice requires us to discern what is spiritual and calls for us to lift ourselves up out of the mundane. Over the last several years, making the virtues of Truth, Beauty, and Goodness my companions at the veil has given me pleasure and a certain amount of wisdom. By getting to know them better—studying them almost as though they are spiritual beings (which they are!)—they have become my teachers, offering reliable guideposts and standards. I strive to understand each virtue's nuances and how together they intertwine and stand as a luminous trinity. I think these virtues are very important to our veil work practice. They can help you recognize communication from loved ones, identify effective spiritual reading materials, and evaluate your co-creative projects.

Philosophical greats including Plato, Aristotle, Thomas Aquinas, Schopenhauer, and Goethe all in some way connected the arts to the virtues of Truth, Beauty, and Goodness and their relationship to a higher power. And I imagine that each spiritual path offers

I strive to understand each virtue's nuances and how together they intertwine and stand as a luminous trinity.

its own unique compass for seeking these virtues, which can be used as a template for your own study. To get you on your way to making these virtues your companions too, let's take a brief look at how three scholars define them.

Historically we can see how today's world has continued, at what feels like an accelerated pace, on the path of what was happening in the 1500s. The 1500s were a turning point in Western civilization, a shift from being God centered to man centered. Howard Gardner, author of *Truth, Beauty, and Goodness Reframed*, speaks to this when he references an essay by historian Henry Adams written in 1904. Gardner writes that "Adams felt inadequate to deal with the many transformations that had taken place since his birth"—among them the growth of cities, mass transportation, scientific breakthroughs, and new technologies. He yearned for society to return to a time and place he saw as representing an ideal. Gardner eloquently summarizes:

> As [Adams] saw it, life in France in the eleventh and twelfth centuries represented an ideal. And that ideal was most dramatically conveyed, indeed embodied, by the magnificent Gothic cathedrals— awe-inspiring buildings where individuals of various backgrounds and classes gathered to worship, to behold splendid works of art, to hear magnificent chorale works, and to be spiritually uplifted. These cathedrals testified to a precious unity in life. The abstract entity—the Church—and its physical realization—the cathedral—represented a world to which all should aspire.

That world was **true**—*directed by the word of God. It was* **beautiful**—*a magnificent construction made by man in the image of God. And it was* **good**—*with the inspiring light of the Church, and the examples of Christ and of the saints, people could and would live a good life.*[1] [emphasis mine]

Though Adams might have preferred it, I am not suggesting that a return to Sunday mass is called for (unless that is your own personal spiritual path), but I do think we all benefit from a conscious integration of the noble virtues he speaks of—Truth, Beauty, and Goodness—into our lives and our practice of veil work.

More contemporarily, author Steve McIntosh, J.D., a leader in the integral (evolutionary) philosophy movement, discusses Truth, Beauty, and Goodness in his books, calling them "the values which guide us into the future."

The ideals of beauty, truth, and goodness represent philosophy's finest hour—these are the concepts by which philosophy makes contact with the spiritual and helps to define the way forward from a middle ground in between science and religion. Indeed, it is in the pursuit of beauty, truth, and goodness that we find the pinnacle of human life. Beauty, truth, and goodness are truly sacred in the way they name and describe the "eternal forms" by which the persuasive influences of evolution enact the universe's essential motion of consciousness seeking its source.[2]

I have found Rudolf Steiner's lecture on these virtues to be the most succinct and the simplest instructions for *how* to integrate them into my life and my veil practice:

To be true is to be rightly united with our spiritual past. To sense beauty means that in the physical world we do not disown our connection with spirit. To be good is to build a living seed for a spiritual world in the future.[3]

When I do my veil practice, I am:

Seeking Spiritual Truth
Embodying the Virtue of Beauty
Enlivening the Art of Goodness

I invite you to do the same.

Veil Work Activities

Identifying the Virtues of Truth, Beauty, and Goodness

Practice discerning whether a poem, a prayer, song lyrics, or other spiritual content has Truth, Beauty, and Goodness at its foundation. This will help you identify these virtues in your co-creative activities.

Truth. Do the words remind you of your spiritual heritage—of being a spiritual being, born out of the spiritual world?

Beauty. Can you feel the words in your selection radiating Spirit?

Goodness. Do the words inspire you to do noble acts that will positively affect the future?

Can you see where these virtues show up in your life now and how you experience them?

Further Reading

Integral Consciousness and the Future of Evolution by Steve McIntosh, Paragon House, 2007.

"Truth, Beauty and Goodness," a lecture by Rudolf Steiner, Dornach, January 19, 1923; see more at: http://wn.rsarchive.org/Lectures/19230119p01.html#sthash.yzCt21J6.dpuf.

Truth, Beauty, and Goodness Reframed: Educating for the Virtues by Howard Gardner, Perseus Books, 2011.

14

Art as a Spiritual Activity

B ecause the arts were such a game changer for me, I would like to bring special attention to them, art as a spiritual activity, and the place of art in your veil work practice. Primarily because of the arts' unique connection to Beauty, they have a special capacity to open our hearts—our feeling realm, which is an essential quality as we approach the veil. If you are not drawn to the typical type of artwork—painting, eurythmy, sculpting, textiles, music, or another form—but would rather express your art through gardening, agriculture, or even in the business world or in a community organization, you can still learn from the principles of determining how art is spiritualized. My intention is that you will be able to transfer these principles to any "art form" that you and your loved one love to do together.

Art and the Soul's Development

There are many way we can start to understand our soul. In this chapter I would like to focus on three aspects of the soul in relationship to art: that the soul is the intermediary between our physical body and our spirit; that the soul carries the forces of thinking, feeling, and willing within it; and that the soul can be ruled by sympathies and antipathies. All of these soul aspects influence the spiritual activity of the art.

Soul as the Intermediary

In his book *Concerning the Spiritual in Art*, Wassily Kandinsky speaks to the powerful connection between art and the development of the soul.

> Painting is an art, and art is not vague production, transitory and isolated, but a power which must be directed to the improvement and refinement of the human soul.... If art refrains from doing this work, a chasm remains unbridged, for no other power can take the place of art in this activity. And at times when the human soul is gaining greater strength, art will also grow in power, for the two are inextricably connected and complementary one to the other. It is very important for the artist to ... search deeply into his own soul, develop and tend it, so that his art has something to clothe, and does not remain a glove without a hand.[1]

The question that Kandinsky leaves us with is how does the artist "search deeply into his own soul, develop and tend it"? Let's allow that question to remain a question in our soul, gently asking our own soul how it would like to be developed and tended to. Only by holding the question ourselves can we ask it of our loved one who has died.

Thinking, Feeling, and Willing

Our soul is also connected to the forces of our thinking, feeling, and willing. It is one of our tasks as human beings to increase our consciousness of how we think, feel, and move through the world as well as to generally harmonize these three forces. As you will learn in the section on the soul's journey after death, when we die the soul and spirit shed the physical body and these three forces start to separate. Increasing our consciousness of the qualities of these soul forces through spiritual art activities provides an education in this, for our loved one and ourselves. When we harmonize our thinking, feeling, and willing aspects, our heart informs our thinking and guides our doing, considering that which is highest for spiritual evolution.

Subjective Versus Objective

At one time I was drawn to practice Aviva Gold's "Painting from the Source" technique. I found it very moving and powerful, yet at the same time it was also subjective: personal to me. This does not mean there was no co-creation with the spiritual world involved in this experience; my loved ones certainly could have inspired me to explore Gold's technique for the particular form of soul healing that it invites. But it is important to discern between these subjective artistic experiences and objective ones.

The subjective calls forth our *own personal sympathy and antipathy* in expressing and experiencing art. Spiritual art, by contrast, *always has relationship to the objective spiritual virtues of Truth, Beauty, and Goodness*. For veil work I recommend choosing an artistic activity that is objective.

Spiritualizing Art Through Truth, Beauty, and Goodness

When the artist recognizes and follows spiritual laws to the best of his or her capacity while creating art, that art will be Truthful. When we create artwork that is Truthful or we see art that is Truthful it reminds us of our spiritual heritage. This ability is directly related to the capacity to discern the Truth in our thinking.

Art that is filled with Beauty radiates spirit, is light filled, and gives us a sense of weight being lifted from our shoulders. Through the act of creating art that is Beauty filled, we claim our place as spiritual beings in a physical world. Beauty both enlivens us and opens our hearts. The awareness of art being filled with Beauty comes through the realm of feeling. Beauty also exists when we transform chaos into something that is harmoniously formed.

Within the third virtue, Goodness, lives a relationship between us and something outside ourselves. Goodness contains a morality that calls for compassion with all that suffers. I believe that when the artist considers the other in the act of creation and in the end product, art itself is a noble act, an act of Goodness, and the resulting art is filled with this virtue.

Spiritual art seeks what is spiritually True during the creation of it, strives to be a source of Beauty through radiating spirit, and stimulates the act of Goodness, creating a spiritual seed that becomes a force of good for the future.

15

Using Color

When we think of the deceased we can help them by
visualizing colors and especially violet—the color that
is so intimately connected with everything that is holy,
with the depth. Colors are soul-substance and that is
something the dead need. Therefore one has to learn to
think in color, without words.
—Liane Collot d'Herbois, *Light, Darkness and Colour in
Painting Therapy*[1]

I t wasn't long after I started reading to Lara and other loved
ones that I received a thought that activated my will, urg-
ing me to pick up my daughter's crayons and color in one
of her coloring books. This was an act of co-creation, granted
unconsciously on my part, but still an act that I acknowledge
looking back. I found moving the crayon across the paper so very
soothing. Even as I relate this experience, I notice that my breathing
changes. An exhale comes that allows my heart to have a sense of
being at ease with what is.

At the same time I began to color with crayons, I started
researching what Rudolf Steiner taught on the subject of color. His
book *Colour*, a series of twelve transcribed lectures, was one of the
first I was led to read.[2] I was also drawn to look for painting classes.

I tried a few, but it wasn't until I was sitting in a class taught by art therapist Iris Sullivan, offered by the Anthroposophical Society in Los Angeles, that I had an "aha moment."

Iris had given the class introductory instructions, and we were all quietly painting "veils"—thin layers of translucent watercolor—onto our paper. Iris was slowly making her way around the class, looking at our work. When I felt Iris behind me looking at my painting, I asked her if the stroke I had just made was "right."

Iris replied, "You can paint it that way, but it would not be lawful."

The word "lawful" resounded in my being. *How can a color be "lawful"?* I thought. The power of that word when used in relationship to color prompted me to explore the concept—yet another dimension of the co-creative activity of working with color—and it still gets my attention today. That is why I wrote the section called Lawful Use of Color you will read next.

I continued painting and developed a new vocation: I sold my paintings at regional art shows in Southern California. When I look back over that time period, I can see that my first impulse to color and my subsequent inspiration to study the spiritual nature of color and become an artist all came from across the threshold. Being led to specific spiritual books to read to my loved ones was the first act of collaboration I experienced. This deep and surprising exploration of color was the second. Although I was always drawn to beauty and color, I do not think it would have occurred to me or I would have desired to explore color or stand at an easel and paint a painting. My mother, as I have mentioned, was the artist in the family, and I never thought I would develop an interest in it myself.

Though I feel my primary co-creative work, with both color and movement, has been through and with Lara and my mother, I have had experiences with others, including a friend's daughter who died at age seventeen. Once I was in the process of completing a painting to send to this friend. It reflected her daughter's transition to the spiritual world and the threshold colors of shades of violet, indigo, and magenta. I was having difficulty with the image and how I thought the painting should look, so I took an image of the painting into my sleep. In the morning as I was coming out of sleep, there was Adele, the daughter. Her name popped into my head and I felt her presence at the foot of my bed, and an image of her as I knew her in the physical realm came naturally to mind. When this happens, it is so joyful! And this was extra special because I could also feel Lara standing beside her. That beautiful moment brings tears to this day. I didn't receive a special "message" from either Adele or Lara; rather, it was a moment in time, a moment of being blessed with the experience and a knowingness of their presence. Later that morning when I met the painting again, through grace, I was able to complete it.

Lawful Use of Color

Let's now discuss the lawful use of color. It is an important concept because it is exactly this lawfulness that makes color spiritual. Working with guidance from Dr. Ita Wegman, artist Liane Collot d'Herbois developed a technique captured in d'Herbois's *Light, Darkness and Colour in Painting Therapy*. Unfortunately, the book is currently out of print, though used copies can be found, and it is worth the search because it contains invaluable information. Here we find a system revealing that each color has a lawful movement, an essential spiritual or soul quality, and a specific effect on human thinking, feeling, and will (behavior). We also learn the spiritual laws of color: how each one is "made" in the spiritual world and is a dance or interplay between the invisible forces of Light and Darkness.

The best way I know to explain the invisible forces of Light and Darkness that d'Herbois describes, and the color that results from them, is to compare them to a common human experience. If you stand outside beside a tree on a moonless night, outside

---

*Each color is "made" in the spiritual world
and is a dance or interplay between
the invisible forces of Light and Darkness.*

---

the range of city lights, you cannot see the tree and its leaves. Though you know the leaves are green, you cannot see the color green. As the first rays of sunlight appear on the horizon, they create form out of what you had only been able to perceive as darkness. Light allows you to see the green of the trees. In the same way, you cannot see color if you are blinded by light. Color and its nuances are displayed only through the interplay between the forces of Light and Darkness: this is a spiritual law of color.

For Spirituality of Color Enthusiasts Only

If, like me, you are excited about the spiritual qualities of color and want to dive deeper into the subject, you will enjoy the following paragraphs and chart. If you prefer to get straight to the Activity section and start experiencing color for yourself, please skip ahead to the section Using Color in Your Veil Work Practice.

Color Influences Our Thinking, Feeling, and Willing
To look at these forces in terms of our human experience, Light is connected to our thinking and Darkness to our will and our actions. The dance of the relationship between the two when they meet is color, and color is connected to our feeling life. Understanding and using the laws of color to create paintings that reflect the true relationships between colors brings harmony and beauty to the viewer of the artwork on all of these levels: in their thinking, doing, and feeling lives. This is why a painting created using spiritual laws

is an act of Goodness that benefits the viewer. There is another level of Goodness as well: the lawful painting creates an unseen force that is a seed for future acts of Goodness.

We innately know the truth of the essential qualities of color. We know about feeling blue, or seeing red. Yet this is a result of our personal sympathies and antipathies, a subjective viewpoint of how a color feels to us personally. Understanding the spiritual nature of colors provides an objective point of view that encourages a balancing, a harmonizing in our soul life that gives us spiritual nourishment, which we in turn can offer to our loved ones.

The nuances of color are particularly relevant because they affect our feelings, our heart's sphere. Our capacity to perceive these nuances has a direct relationship to our ability to feel alive. It's fun to use the analogy of coloring. If you were given the choice between a box of eight Crayola crayons or a box of sixty-four, which do you think would offer the liveliest experience of coloring? Those sixty-four crayons will move your soul in sixty-four different ways because of the sixty-four different spiritual essences they carry. The world of color is the world of the soul—it warms the heart.

Our Angels Love Our Connection to Color

Color is very much connected to the angelic realms. In fact, it is actually a deed of the realm of the Third Hierarchy. As Rudolf Steiner said:

> These Angels [angels, archangels, and archai] bore light into the darkness, or darkness into the light. They became the mediators and messengers between light and darkness. And what had previously only shone in the light and brought its shadow, the air darkness, after it, now burst into colour, changing from one colour to another, as the light appeared in the darkness and the darkness in the light. It is the Third Hierarchy who conjured forth colours out of light and darkness.[3]

Because of this deep connection between the Third Hierarchy of angels and color, I believe that studying and working with color pleases our own personal guardian angels and provides a door to enriching our connection with these spiritual helpers.

Color and Wellness

Next I would like to present a table I created to compare the philosophies of Johann Wolfgang von Goethe; Rudolf Steiner; and Liane Collot d'Herbois and Ita Wegman, who worked together on the effects of color on the wellness of the human being in relation to thinking, feeling, and willing.

We begin on the left with Goethe, whose *Theory of Colours*, a study of the relationship of light, darkness, and color, represents a milestone in color theory. Building upon this is Steiner's distinction of the thinking, feeling, and willing aspects of the human being; he gave indications of their connection to the physiology of the human being. Next, Collot d'Herbois and Wegman developed guidelines for working with specific colors, their "movement," and their application to different areas of the canvas as a therapeutic modality for the physiology of the human being: specifically the nervous, rhythmic, and metabolic systems. Finally, I have overlaid these findings with their connection to the spiritual qualities of Truth, Beauty, and Goodness.

Goethe (1749-1832)	Steiner (1961-1925)	Collot d'Herbois (1907-99) and Wegman (1876-1943)	Spiritual Virtue
Light	Thinking and the nervous system	Specific colors and their movements applied in the upper region of a painting for affecting thinking and the nervous system	Truth
Color	Feeling and the rhythmic system	Specific colors and their movements applied in the middle region of a painting for affecting feeling and the rhythmic system	Beauty
Darkness	Willing (behavior) and the metabolic system	Specific colors and their movements applied in the lower region of a painting for affecting the will (behavior) and the metabolic system	Goodness

Using Color in Your Veil Work Practice

Color has been and continues to be an integral part of my spiritual service to Lara and other loved ones. I have found that color is a wonderful way to offer spiritual nourishment, and using color for this purpose does not require any formal training or particular skill level, so it is perfect for your veil work practice. All you need is the intention to serve your loved one and a willingness to play and explore the ways in which color can enrich this spiritual practice. The best way to learn this visual form of communication with your loved one is by doing, and I have created several activities for you. If you are feeling a little resistance to playing with color—or a lot—select at least one color activity to do each week for four weeks, and see what color invites between you and your loved one.

Veil Work Activities

Orange Crayons

Sit with two boxes of crayons: one with eight shades and one with sixty-four. Find the "true orange" in the box of eight. In the box of sixty-four, gather the true orange and all the shades of orange. Place all these orange crayons in front of you. Color a blank white sheet of paper with the crayons, starting with the true orange and going through each shade of orange. Now re-create the image of each color in your mind's eye and infuse it with a feeling of the color. Picture yourself offering each of the colors to your loved one. How does each color make you feel? See if you can sense how your loved one received each color—did you sense a different reaction with the true orange as compared to all its shades? Looking at the true orange, can you find a connection to courage? Write your findings in your journal.

Darkness and Light

It is powerful to note that perceiving darkness does not hurt, while being blinded by light does hurt. Why do you think or feel this is so? Note your observations in your journal.

Sunrise/Sunset

At sunrise or sunset, go to a place in nature where you can observe the sky. Note the play of colors. As the colors in the sky and on the surrounding landscape shift, periodically capture a living image in your mind and offer it to your loved one so they might see the colors as you do. Sense how your loved one felt receiving this image from you. When you get home, write your experience in your journal.

Threshold Watercolor Painting

This activity will use color to help you approach the threshold between you and your loved one. You will use light and dark shades of the color violet. Start by reviewing the spiritual qualities of these colors. Contemplate these qualities for a few moments before you begin. The qualities originated with Liane Collot d'Herbois.

Spiritual Qualities of Light Violet

Light violet leads us *across* the threshold into the spiritual world. It contains qualities of selflessness, gratitude, and the "washing of the feet" principle—to serve one another lovingly and humbly. It also helps in overcoming egoism.

Spiritual Qualities of Violet

Violet is intimately connected with everything that is holy. It holds qualities of self-sacrifice—it demands something from us. When we allow violet to penetrate to the very core of who we are, we are still and at peace. It is a color that takes us to the threshold of the spiritual world. You can find violet in nature in amethyst, pansies, or irises.

Art Supplies

- Violet watercolor pigment: two variations of violet, light and dark. I can recommend for light violet Winsor & Newton Cotman Mauve #398 and for the dark violet, Winsor & Newton Cotman Dioxazine Violet #231.
- Watercolor paper, or drawing paper (60 lbs. and greater), 11" x 14"
- A one-inch brush (inexpensive goat hair)
- Two painting pots or dishes

Step-by-Step Instructions

When you do this exercise, work in a gentle movement from above to below, like softly falling snow, starting each new stroke at the top of the page.

Bring in your loved one, using whatever method works best for you.

Squeeze a small dab (the size of a pea) of each paint color into its own pot or dish. Enjoy the rich, deep pigment as it comes out of the tube.

Dilute the two pigments with water.

Breathe in the colors, noting how each color makes you feel. Visualize the two violet colors to your loved one.

Turn your paper "portrait style," with the short edges at top and bottom.

Either using your imagination or by drawing very lightly, mark off a "door" or passageway in the center of your paper, about 5 to 6 inches tall and 3 to 3½ inches wide. Start at the upper left side of the sheet of paper and paint slowly downward with the light violet, painting with the quality of softly falling snow. Paint all the way across the piece of paper, even over your door.

Let this first wash of light violet watercolor dry.

Next, using the dark violet, start at the upper left side and paint in the same way, over the layer of light violet from the top to the bottom, very slowly. This time, do not paint over the "door" in your painting.

Let this wash of dark violet watercolor dry.

Now apply another layer of dark violet, but with this layer of wash, stop short of the door by about an inch or so.

Allow this wash to dry.

Continue applying layers of the dark violet wash only, with each layer stopping short of the last layer by about an inch.

The effect should be that you feel pulled into the threshold by the contrast of the light violet door and the darker violet veils around the door.

Meditate on this painting and see yourself meeting your loved one at the door. Journal any resistance or eagerness you have for meeting your loved one at the door.

Nice job! Know that all these activities provide your loved one with spiritual nourishment.

Further Reading

Colour: Twelve Lectures by Rudolf Steiner, Rudolf Steiner Press, 1996.

16

Eurythmy: Movement That Penetrates The Veil

The mother stated that of all activities, eurythmy
brought her the closest to her deceased child.
—Carol Ann Williamson, therapeutic eurythmist*

Eurythmy is artistic movement. In practicing it, the eurythmist
embodies the sounds of speech or the tones and intervals of
music, primarily through arm gestures. Each sound of the
words of a poem and each tone and interval of a musical composition
is filled with creative forces that originate in the spiritual world.
When we express with our limbs the creative power that lives in
the individual sounds and originates in the cosmos, it spiritualizes
movement.

This is what makes eurythmy so unique and so important for
today's world. The practice directly connects us with the spiritual
creative powers where our loved one lives, and this "lights us up" to

---

*This mother's young child had died in a car accident. Williamson
supported her through eurythmy sessions, mainly leading her in the
eurythmy Hallelujah gestures, followed by quiet time.

When we express with our limbs the creative power that lives in the individual sounds and originates in the cosmos, it spiritualizes movement.

---

our loved one, enabling them to see us. Not only that, but it gives them the opportunity to engage in an artistic activity together with us. Powerful! This is why eurythmy is such an excellent practice for veil work.

Eurythmy Harmonizes Thinking, Feeling, and Willing

Even though eurythmy started out as a performance art, its underpinnings for the healing of mankind were always there. This is why its reach broadened from stage performance to a place at the heart of the curriculum of Waldorf Education, a component of healthy organizations, and a significant element of Anthroposophic medicine.

In fact, a whole field of therapeutic eurythmy arose. A eurythmist may receive additional training and work in conjunction with a medical doctor who prescribes specific eurythmy exercises for the client.

> In the sphere of healing Curative Eurythmy works in the first place as the great harmoniser, bringing the powers of the soul, thinking, feeling and willing, into their proper relationship with the three systems of the body on which they are based, the head, rhythmic and limb systems, and strengthening that balance between earthly and cosmic forces through which man realises his true egohood.[1]

My Road to Eurythmy

As I share my story of how I came to be a eurythmist, I invite you to practice thinking about your own co-creative moments, times when your loved ones who have died might have influenced your actions.

When eurythmy first came into my life, I had no clue about its spiritual significance to those who have died. I told you a little bit about my first experience with eurythmy in chapter 8 on receiving communication through the veil. I can still vividly recall seeing eurythmy live for the first time, performed by Truus Geraets, a therapeutic eurythmist, and several other eurythmists on an intimate stage at the Los Angeles branch of the Anthroposophical Society in Pasadena. I cannot say that there was anything extraordinary about the performance that evening, though I am sure it was lovely. What left a lasting impression on me was the sight of Truus moving diagonally from the back of the stage to the front, stage right, and doing the sound *I*. She was wearing a green eurythmy dress the color of spring leaves, and I was pulled into the movement. It was one of those pivotal moments that at the time I didn't recognize, but it certainly became a destiny moment for me.

I had been on track to get a degree in physical therapy and had been accepted into the highly selective Western States Physical Therapy Program for the fall 2001 term. But the second week, while sitting in one of my PT classes, I received a clear message: *this is not for you.* The following week I found myself un-enrolling from the PT program. It wasn't a decision I took lightly, but I had to honor what I knew to be true for myself, whatever the consequences.

Feeling a bit at a loss as to what to do with my life now, and since I enjoyed movement, I began one-on-one eurythmy sessions with Truus. I had no notion of pursuing a eurythmy diploma then—it was not even on my radar.

I had been working with Truus in individual sessions for about six months when she suggested that I take a week-long eurythmy course for the public—a nonprofessional training—that was being held at Eurythmy Spring Valley in Chestnut Ridge, New York. Most of this course was uncomfortable for me. I felt awkward and out of place. Added to this was the fact that the way eurythmy is taught activated a slight disconnect that my brain happens to have between hearing a sound and trying to name it, something similar to what's called "auditory processing disorder." My brain had to take an extra step that most people do not need to take. I have always had a hard time pronouncing words, sounding out their phonetics and recognizing how they are spelled. When I was a child this was duly noted on my report card with specific instructions: "Lynn is to read out loud at home." My second grade teacher would be impressed that I am still reading out loud at home!

The Frontier Eurythmy Program

Despite my overall feelings of inadequacy, in January 2003 I found myself back on campus enrolled in the Frontier Eurythmy program, a new professional training track offered especially for people who could not enroll full time. What changed my mind? During that first week-long course I met some really terrific women who *loved* eurythmy. One of them emailed me to ask if I was going to enroll, and that gave me pause. I was torn: I didn't really want to do it, yet some feeling inside of me was telling me it was exactly what I should do. When I got off the fence, I sent in my application and tuition money and I began the new year with a group of wonderful women and some of the best eurythmy teachers in the world—still feeling like a fish out of water, and yes, afraid.

How did this happen? Two specific indications tell me that, like my impulse to explore color, this was a co-creative activity, guidance that came not from within but directly from my loved ones across the veil. The first indication was that my own internal compass never gave me an absolute "Yes! Go to eurythmy school!"

Instead, most mornings when I walked to school I simply felt a strong message from Lara and others: "Just do it today, just this day." This encouragement continued through years of part-time and full-time study until I graduated and received my diploma in June 2009.

A Blessing of Grace

By the time I entered eurythmy school, I had already been reading to Lara and my other loved ones for a little over four years. Even though we don't do this work for blessings, I do have to note that I was reaping the blessings of that practice. I felt about Lara and my loved ones what Rudolf Steiner described about a colleague of his who had died. He felt her presence during artistic performances that he and others were doing in Munich, Germany: "I was always aware that this individual was looking down on everything that is happening. It is, of course, not true that such a being would tell us how to do things. We must have our own abilities for that. But through the blessing flowing to us from such an individual, we can feel strengthened for the task at hand. We can feel her radiant spiritual eye and her warm, sincere interest flowing into the things we have to do."[2]

In addition to this constant, loving support, which I received on a feeling level, I received an infusion of physical energy that gave me staying power. Again, this was not my own internal reservoir of strength—it was a transfer of the extra life forces Lara had to offer because she had died prematurely. I learned firsthand that when human beings die in childhood they have unspent energy they can transfer to the living. I saw this demonstrated through a collaborative act, and I have no doubt that without that extra life force, I would not have had the stamina or resilience necessary to complete a training that was so uncomfortable for me and required such a strong, sustained commitment. As Albert Steffen wrote in

Meetings with Rudolf Steiner, "Those dying young carry back into the spiritual world the cosmic element that lives in the unspent forces of growth [etheric forces]—something divine that has not yet been corroded and destroyed by earthly consciousness."[3]

On the Other Side of the Training

I don't know if I will ever fully understand during my lifetime the nature of my destiny path of becoming a eurythmist and the spiritual commitments I made to Lara. I do know that Lara had physical disabilities, and Rudolf Steiner has said that when certain skills or capacities are held back, these forces can become potent for future use. I don't know if this is true in Lara's case, but I feel an inner warmth, a quiet joy, from knowing our eurythmy co-creation could enhance her quality of movement in her next incarnation.

Now that I am on the other side of eurythmy training, I am grateful, and I feel blessed by the gift of eurythmy in my life. As a professional eurythmist I bring eurythmy to adults and organizations, and in my veil work practice I bring eurythmy to my loved ones who have died. It truly is a co-creative endeavor. And because eurythmy has the power to return us to a unique spiritual awareness in a community experience, I believe it is *the* social art that is most sorely needed during these times of uncertainty and global unrest.

Diving Deeper

If you want to delve further into understanding the spiritual qualities of eurythmy and its connection to the creative forces contained within words, read on. If you would prefer to get started in some eurythmy practices, you can skip ahead to the Activities section on page 217.

If you are staying with me, we will start where the story begins: the time when an impulse to spiritualize dance emerged.

Origins of Eurythmy: In the Beginning Was the Word

In the early 1900s there was an impulse to spiritualize dance. Three dancers—Isadora Duncan, Ruth St. Denis, and Maud Allan—were among those to take the lead in exploring how this could be done. For some of the dancers of that era, the search for the spirit in movement was a response to the materialism that was encroaching on the world they knew. Modern dance was one form that rose from this exploration.

Rudolf Steiner often said that it was the destiny of Henri Smits's death that led to the beginnings of eurythmy.[4] It was mid-December 1911. Clara Smits's husband had died unexpectedly the month before from a heart attack. Now she was meeting with Rudolf Steiner, a family friend, in Berlin, seeking advice on what profession her nineteen-year-old daughter, Lory, could enter. While she sat in the waiting room preparing to speak with Steiner, she overheard a conversation between two people about movement. She mentioned this conversation during her meeting with Steiner, adding that Lory "loved to move." He told her that he would be glad to teach Lory a system of dance that was inspired by spirit and affirmed to her that this movement would be life-giving and initiate a healing process within the human being.[5]

Rudolf Steiner was not interested in revamping any current or past systems of dance. Rather, he wanted to develop a dance form that was entirely inspired by spirit and accessible to contemporary consciousness, striving for ego awareness and individualization. Eurythmy is an excellent tool for self-knowledge and for teaching how to self-individualize while also being in community. He believed that such a system of movement would need to be based on the sounds of speech—the spiritual power of the word. As Marjorie Raffe et al. noted in their book on eurythmy:

It was perhaps typical of Steiner that, when asked about the revival of the dance, he replied that anyone who wanted to acquire a pure conception of the quality of movement should study the sounds of speech. For speech is one of the greatest of human mysteries. It is the human microcosm of the macrocosmic Logos or Creative Word—the speaking of the Divine powers in the act of creation to which all religions refer. Eurythmy begins, then, with the more difficult task of interpreting speech in movement—and then passes over to the more traditional and accepted task of doing the same with music.[6]

The intimate connection between words and movement may not be immediately obvious or intuitive, but if you want to become acquainted with eurythmy, it is important to see them as parts of an expressive whole. Let's take a moment to reflect on the nature of words.

The Word
A word is dead
When it is said,
Some say.
I say it just
Begins to live
That day.
—Emily Dickinson (1830–86)

Emily Dickinson wrote more than seventeen hundred poems and ten thousand pieces of correspondence during her lifetime. She knew the power of the word—the *living* power and creative force that is contained within the sounds of words. I find this poem an excellent expression of that understanding.

What Happens When We Speak

You can think of the spoken word as a gesture we place in the air. Just as when we throw a pebble into a pond, the resulting ripples travel across the water, our words ripple outward too. When we speak a word, our larynx, mouth, and lips press the air into certain invisible gestures that are powered by our thoughts and feelings and carried through the air. These air gestures cause vibrations that are audible to our ears and that our brains interpret.

In eurythmy we imitate the air gestures that our organs of speech form, embodying the sounds, primarily using the limbs, especially the arms. Thus eurythmy truly is "visible speech." But there is an invisible component too: the goal of the eurythmist is to embody the sound so completely that the embodiment extends throughout every cell of their being.

Knowledge of the Creative Power of Words Is Universal

Author Richard Rudd writes in *Gene Keys: Unlocking the Higher Purpose Hidden in Your DNA:*

> There is deep magic woven into language. It is why the origin of the word "spell" correlates with the idea of casting spells that have power over others. Every word has an inner spirit—a code of light that lends it an independent force in the cosmos. The moment a word or group of words is given voice, vibrations radiate out into the universe. There is no return.[7]

Speaking of spells, one of my favorite words is *abracadabra*. We can intuitively sense that there is magic in it. It is Aramaic in origin: *abra* means "to create" and *cadabra* translates "as I say," so the word literally means "create as I say"—an affirmation that the spoken word is in itself a creative force.

Now let's consider the *mantra*, a word meaning "thought form" with origins in the ancient Sanskrit language of India. Goswami Kriyananda writes:

> Mantras are sacred formulas or mystical verses that contain within them primary vibratory forces that create mystical states of consciousness.... Some mystics say that these mystical states of consciousness can manifest in the external world. All sounds made by earthlings carry a mental influence which exerts itself over matter, whether or not the earthling perceives it. [8]

This definition reaffirms my own experience with eurythmy. I have long believed that every time someone does eurythmy with a pure heart, an invisible substance of will is created that can then be translated into heart-based action.

Mantras are often used as prayers or hymns—a word or sequence of words that embody and invoke the Divine. Repeating a mantra again and again harnesses its magical power. The mantra that many of us are familiar with is *om*, which is often described as the "cosmic sound" or the "sound of the universe." The first verse of the *Mandukya Upanishad*, an ancient writing whose main theme is the mystic word *om*, states:

> OM! This Imperishable Word is the whole of this visible universe. Its explanation is as follows: What has become, what is becoming, what will become—verily, all of this is OM. And what is beyond these three states of the world of time—that too, verily, is OM. [9]

Moving from Hinduism to Judaism now, we have the Hebrew word *davar*, a word meaning *word* as well as *action* and *thing*.

The Davar became flesh ... and we gazed upon his glory:

I have long believed that every time someone does eurythmy with a pure heart, an invisible substance of will is created that can then be translated into heart-based action.

---

the One and Only of a father, full of steadfast love and truth.... In Hebrew Scripture the noun *Davar* has dual meaning clusters: (1) what is spoken, and (2) what is done. *Davar* denotes a word, promise, message, report, oracle, or plan. Or it denotes a thing or reality: that is, a thing that is done, a deed, an action.[10]

In the Christian Bible, the prologue from the Gospel of Saint John speaks to the creative living power within the word:

In the beginning was the Word, the Word was with God and the Word was God. He was with God in the beginning. Through Him all things came to be, not one thing had its being but through Him.[11]

These are some classical examples that reflect ancient understandings of the power of the word. Today, some common expressions demonstrate our innate understanding that we can create through our words. "You have my word on it" and "I give you my word" mean "I have said it and I will make it so." Though one might argue that within the animal kingdom some forms of language exist, the intricacy of speech is truly a unique capacity of the human being. Yet the ability to create through our words is in danger of becoming a lost art. This is another reason eurythmy is such a valuable practice right now; it reconnects us to this profound human capacity.

What Is a Word?

What is a word? Why does it hold creative power? Let's break it down.

In a word we have the sounds of vowels and consonants sequenced in a particular pattern. The sequencing of the sounds is the "architectural plan" for creating the thing that the word names.

Let me give you an example. We intuitively know that the word *house* feels different from the word *home*. If I asked you to draw a picture of a house and beside it a picture of a home, what specific details would each drawing have? You might draw the house in a streamlined way—a simple, bare-bones structure. Your home, on the other hand, might include curtains in the window, a tree in the front yard, smoke softly rising out of the chimney, and a family walking up to the front door. It would probably have a much warmer quality. If we look at the two words—house, home—we find that they contain similar sounds: they both begin with H, they both contain an O, and they both end in an E. The differences are that in house the O is combined with a U, forming the diphthong OU, and there is an S in the word. With home, there is simply an O sound and an M. If we look at just two sounds with insights from eurythmy, we can start to feel into why *house* builds a different image in our minds from *home*. The sound of *s* denotes strength and mastery; we certainly want our house to be strong and know that it was built with a level of mastery. With the sound of *m* we penetrate into the other—we take part of the other into ourselves and give part of ourselves to the other. There is a level of intimacy with the *m* that offers an image of a home we share with others.

Naming Sounds

Our ancestors knew how important sounds were—so important, in fact, that they actually named them. For example, the Hebrews named the sound *ah* "Aleph." "The Aleph symbolizes the One and Only, the Eternal, the Omnipotent God. It is the symbol of God as the Creator and Master of the universe."[12] David Sacks writes:

According to mystical writings such as the medieval European compilation called the Kabalah, *alef* symbolizes the Divine energy that preceded and initiated Creation. This seeding power existed before any other form could be realized, which is why the opening word of the Hebrew Bible—*bereshith* ("in the beginning") starts with the Hebrew alphabet's second letter, not the first.[13]

When you understand the primal nature of the *ah* sound, you can then comprehend why A is the first letter in our alphabet and why *ah* is typically the first sound a baby makes. The Greeks were the last civilization to name sounds: the word for *ah* in Greek is "alpha," meaning "being in the state of constant activity, of becoming."[14]

To begin to explore what Steiner is describing, if we consciously feel into the sound of *ah*, we will have a soul experience of the essential qualities of *ah*: astonishment and wonder. As Steiner observes, "Philosophy, the love of wisdom, the love of knowledge, begins with wonder." If I say and feel into the sound of *b* "it is always something wrapping. A protecting, sheltering form would be produced."[15] Something would be produced which might be likened to a hut or a house. We can feel this sense of enclosure when we say the words *body, bud, bottle*. Each of these sounds—and the sounds of every vowel and consonant in the alphabet—has essential qualities that the dead can "read" and understand.

Our Modern Use of Words

We use language as a bridge between ourselves and others in our society. We use words to communicate logical and intellectual knowledge as well as to express our feelings. Today, two trends are on the rise that have changed how we write and speak words, and thus our ability to connect with the spiritual basis of words.

Because we are trying to keep up with a very fast and busy world, today when we write we abbreviate words and create acronyms for series of words; reducing "in my opinion" to IMO is one example.

The truncating of words is even making its way into our speech—
"LOL" for "laughing out loud" can be spoken as well as written.
Habitual texting and Twittering reinforce this truncating trend.

Our capacity to speak clearly is being diminished as well because
people are increasingly choosing to communicate in writing using
electronic methods with shortened words and phrases instead of
speaking with one another. You may have been with family members
or friends who decide to text each other even when they are together
in the same room—or you may have done that yourself!

From our brief review of our ancestors' wisdom about the sounds
of words as creative forces—knowledge we share cross-culturally—
you can easily see that these trends are not serving us. They are
actually harming us by cutting us off from the direct connection
with the power of creation and the Divine.

The same trend of truncating our language is weakening our
imaginations—a key capacity that we need in order to solve prob-
lems. We no longer "see" or imagine the distinction between a
house and a home when we use the words interchangeably, when
we do not bring conscious awareness to what the proper word for
a particular situation is. This makes our thinking less flexible and
renders our feeling life less deep and colorful and more black and
white.

For most of us, sounds and words have become abstract concepts.
Hebrew leaders knew that our heritage of the sounds of words rested
in the Divine. They understood the living creative power that
lived within the sounds. When they sounded a word, they were
conscious of the Divine speaking within their souls and creating
through them. But beginning with the Romans, this knowledge
and experience began to drop from human consciousness.

Successful leaders from all aspects of life—art, spirituality,
politics, education, business—still understand and make use of the
power of words. Some even understand the connection between
sounds and the Divine. But the whole of society has lost touch
with this. This is where incorporating eurythmy into your veil work

comes in. By reconnecting with the dormant power permeating each sound, understanding the sounds, and feeling their connection to the Divine, you are able to offer these as nourishment to your loved ones and your loved ones can find you more easily.

Vibrating the Word—Cosmic Origins

A thought, powered by our feelings, is expressed through sound: "For a man's words flow out of what fills his heart." (Matthew 12:34–35) The spiritual force that accompanies the sound is the *etheric force*: a life-giving force similar to the life force that we find in plants. It is related to the etheric body, the subtle energetic body that contains the forces that maintain our shape.

What are these Divine, creative life forces in the sounds of words and where do they come from? There is a cosmic connection. The vowels are related to planetary forces. As the planets move in the heavens, the vowels sound their music. The consonants are connected with the fixed constellations of the zodiac. Combined, these heavenly forces give specific powers to sounds. The sounds have an essence of their own, and that essence is colored by a planet or constellation.

The following table shows correlations between vowels and their sounds, and the planets and their influences on the human being. It also includes the colors associated with the planets. Next is a table that correlates the consonants with constellations of the zodiac and their influences.

Vowel	Quality of the Vowel Sound	Planet	Color Mood Associated with Planet	Planetary Influences on the Human Being
A (ah)	Wonder; astonishment	Venus	Green— both spring green and viridian	Loving, devoted
E (long a)	To be affected by something and to withstand it	Mars	Red	Capacity for aggression
I (long ee)	Here I am; positive self-assertion	Mercury	Yellow	Individual-ization
O (long o)	Embracing some-one we love	Jupiter	Orange	Wisdom
U (oo)	Coming back into oneself; a certain amount of chill and rigidness	Saturn	Indigo	Inward; contemplation
AU (ou)	One has a know-ingness of oneself and the world	Sun	White	The whole human being
AI	Attaching oneself; adhering; becoming intimate	Moon	Violet	Creative capacity

Consonant	The Quality of the Sound of the Consonant	Zodiac Constellation and Its Influences on the Human Being
T	Spirit streaming down from above	Leo; enthusiasm, feeling
D	All that descends	Leo; enthusiasm, feeling
B	Protection, enclosure	Virgo; sobriety (reality check)
P	Gesture full of dignity and greatness	Virgo; sobriety (reality check)

C (ts, as in dance)	Raises matter into the realm of the spirit, models light-ness	Libra; a weighing up of a thought
S	Consists of a powerful peace-bringing element, bringing calm and peace into that which is in a state of unrest; mastery	Scorpio; thinking
G	Self-strengthening; the thought that would like to become reality	Sagittarius; the thought that wishes to be turned into reality, resolve
K	Clearing away, breaking up; the thought that would like to become reality	Sagittarius; the thought that wishes to be turned into reality, resolve
L	Creative; form-giving element	Capricorn; thought coming to terms with the outer world
M	Entering right into something	Aquarius; human being finding the balance of the thinking, feeling, will-ing within
N	Touch and release	Pisces; the event has become destiny
V	Feels the need to wander	Aries; the deed has been accomplished, the event
W	This is the sound that bears the waves, that has onward movement on its back	Aries; the deed has been accomplished, the event
R	Something that lies midway between the yielding-up of oneself and self-assertion	Taurus; the deed, will
H	The process of wafting, moving buoyantly, lightly on air toward you	Gemini; capacity for deeds, action
F	"Know, then, that I know"; When somebody thorough-ly knows a thing	Cancer; impulse toward a deed

Source: Rudolf Steiner's *Eurythmy as Visible Speech*.

I would like to share a passage from one of Rudolf Steiner's lectures to connect these tables to veil work. It speaks to how the dead "read":

> Between death and a new birth, we use the stars as a kind of text … How do we read here on Earth? We have approximately twelve consonants and seven vowels with various variations. We arrange these letters in many ways into words. Think how a typesetter mixes the letters together in order to form words: all the words consist of the specific letters that we possess. For the dead, the fixed stars of the zodiac and the planets are what letters are for us here on the physical plane. The fixed stars of the zodiac are the consonants, and the planets are the vowels … the dead can read what lies spiritually at the foundation of the stars.[16]

One of the many things I love about eurythmy is that it opens the heart, something that is sorely needed in the world today when there is so much suffering that tempts us to close our hearts. Another aspect I love is that eurythmy is for everyone. Rudolf Steiner affirmed this when he said, "When asked at what age a person can do eurythmy, I have always said that there are no age limits. From three until the age of ninety, the personality can fully find its place in eurythmy, for every period of life can reveal its beauties in eurythmy."[17] It is valuable for infants and babies to see adults perform these movements. Eurythmy is a reminder for young and old of our own Truth, Beauty, and Goodness: our spiritual heritage.

Now it is time to experience eurythmy in your body.

Veil Work Activities—Eurythmy Gestures and Exploratory Exercises

Please note: eurythmy is not done in front of a mirror.

I Think Speech
The following six positions are designed to help our bodies become instruments of speaking (speech eurythmy). You might try drawing them first—using stick figures is fine—in your journal.

Stand upright. Feel the weight of your body over the balls of your feet. Your knees are soft and your arms are at your sides.

Position 1: I Think Speech
Lift your arms up to the side until they are level with your shoulders, at about a 90 degree angle relative to your spine.

Position 2: I Speak
Now lift your arms a little higher so you could draw a straight line from the vocal cords area of your throat to the tips of your fingers. At the same time, take your right foot to the right about six inches.

Position 3: I Have Spoken
Lower your arms so that your fingertips align with your heart. Picture a line extending from the fingertips of your right hand straight through your heart to the fingertips of your left hand. At the same time, take your left foot out about six to ten inches so your feet are about shoulder width apart.

Position 4: I Seek Myself in the Spirit
Open your arms and legs to the widest positions, with the right foot leading the foot movement, making a large X with your entire body. Feel the wide expanses of the heavens above you and the Earth below.

Position 5: I Feel Myself Within myself (or I Feel myself Within Myself)
Lower your arms so your fingertips are even with the top of your head and bring your feet back to shoulder width apart, with the left foot leading the movement. A line drawn from your left fingertips to your right fingertips would run across the top of your head.

Position 6: I Am on the Way to the Spirit to Myself
Lift your arms overhead, parallel to each other, while bringing your feet together, the right foot leading the movement. Imagine yourself as a beam of light reaching up to the heavens while your feet remain solidly on the ground.

End the sequence by bringing your arms down to the sides of your body. Stay in a moment of silence.

The I-A-O

This is a great activity to do every day. Perform the sequence three times. For this movement, the I sounds like a long *ee*, the A sounds like *ah*, and the O sounds like a long *o*.

I *(ee)*: Stand upright with soft knees, arms relaxed at your sides. The weight of your body rests on the balls of your feet. Feel the movement starting from the sternum/heart area of your chest. Stretch your right arm diagonally up and to the right out in front of your body. At the same time your left arm extends diagonally down and to the left and back just past your body. There is no need to overstretch. This movement is the sound I *(ee)*. Let your body speak it—you do not need to use your voice. Allow yourself a feeling of: "Here I am."

Now release your I *(ee)*.

A (sounds like *ah*): Stand upright with soft knees, arms relaxed at your sides. Feel the movement starting from the sternum/heart area of your chest. Extend your arms out in front of you at an angle, approximately at shoulder height, and making about a 90-degree angle from your spine. Let the weight of your body come back slightly onto your heels. Allow yourself a feeling of wonder and amazement while letting your body speak this gesture of A *(ah)*.

Now release your A *(ah)*.

O (long *o*): Stand upright with soft knees, arms relaxed at your sides. Feel the movement starting from the sternum/ heart area of your chest. Make a gesture of O (circle) in front of you with your arms at shoulder height, fingers touching. Let the weight of your body come forward slightly onto your toes. Allow yourself a feeling of devotion and love while letting your body speak this gesture of O.

Lory's First Lesson

On January 29, 1912, Rudolf Steiner gave Lory Maier-Smits her first eurythmy lesson, and she became the very first eurythmist. However, Steiner did not give her any movements to do. Instead, he gave her a list of instructions. Here are three of them for your own practice.

- Learn about the human body, especially the bones, joints, muscles, and ligaments necessary for movement.
- Observe what happens in your throat as you speak sentences that only have a single vowel: How Now Brown Cow.
- Write with your feet in mirror-writing—the way the words would look in a mirror. Hints: Hold the pencil between your big toe and next toe. Sheets of newsprint paper, 24" x 36", work great for this.

Why do you think Steiner gave these instructions to Lory?

Great job! With these practices added to the eurythmy activities you did in chapters 2 and 6, you have begun to learn what it feels like to speak using your body as an instrument. This is the creative power of sound, spoken in a language that your loved one can easily see.

Part 6

An Imagining of the Soul's Journey

As I related in the very first chapter of this book, one of my main motivations for developing a veil work practice was that I wanted to know where my daughter was and what she was doing, now that she had left her earthly body and was traveling in spiritual realms. I have devoted a great deal of time and study to answering those questions since I first pursued that intention. Again, I followed Rudolf Steiner's lead, reading his writings and those of others who are also students of Steiner. In order to answer those questions for you and to give you an imagining of where your loved ones are traveling and what they are learning there, I have summarized in the next two chapters many of the insights I gained. Chapter 17 covers the first part of the after-death journey—the soul realms of the spiritual world. Then, in chapter 18, the journey continues with expansion into what Steiner terms *spirit country*, the realms of pure spirit and the home of the Divine.

Before you dive in, I would like to emphasize that everything you are about to read is the result of deep exploration of my own spiritual path of esoteric Christianity. If your path is different, I simply ask that you receive this information with an open heart.

17

The Journey Through the Soul Worlds: Purification

Be a star that does not diminish the sacred dark through
which it shines. Be the sun, and illuminate a world.
—Mary Stewart Adams, star lore historian[1]

There is a reason that when we look up to the starry heavens
on a clear night, we are in awe of the majesty that is displayed before us: our gaze is resting upon our spiritual home.

As a spiritual researcher, I have learned to depend on my inner
guidance system to determine whether a specific spiritual teaching
or practice is in alignment with my spiritual path and goals. I trust
you feel the same. From my perspective, it takes an *initiate*—someone
who has been directly initiated into the spiritual realms—to be
able to view and describe the spiritual journey after death. In my
studies I have found that many people have written books and/
or have channeled information and experiences of parts of the
journey. They discuss the three-day review experience, releasing
the etheric body, and the soul space of the spiritual world where we
purify and release the astral body—what some traditional religions
might call purgatory, more esoteric paths might term Kamaloka, or
as Rudolf Steiner also describes it, the "Moon sphere." I have yet

225

to read an author who like Rudolf Steiner describes the spiritual worlds past this purification period. This does not mean that there are not people out there who can. I just have not been exposed to their work or writings.

Of all the resources I have come across, Rudolf Steiner's descriptions of what happens after we die best resonate with me. As a student of his work, I can only share with you what I have gleaned from his writings and lectures at my own level of spiritual understanding. Even though, through meditative practices, I have at times come close to leaving my body for the purpose of experiencing the spirit world myself, I still have not achieved this level of skill. This means that I am left to interpret Steiner's writings on the subject. I appreciate that he has written about it from myriad perspectives, and I marvel at his ability to describe the spiritual worlds using the words of humans on Earth, which I am sure are inadequate for that task.

I also take extremely seriously the fact that coming across Steiner's unique body of spiritual teachings just six months prior to Lara's death was an important destiny meeting for me. Steiner always said that no one should just take his word for it and that each of us are to do our own spiritual research, and I have done the best I can with that advice considering that I am not myself a spiritual initiate.

At the end of the activities section of this chapter, I list several of Steiner's books that speak to the soul's journey. He identifies the journey as a planetary one, and I will use his planetary references while also bringing to light some of the essential qualities of the soul's journey. Another reference I have used is *Citizens of the Cosmos* by Beredene Jocelyn, who spent a lifetime studying Steiner's work.

My goals for this chapter are to give you a clear picture of where your loved one is and what they might be experiencing, while at the same time preparing you for your own journey to the spiritual world. As I have said before, we are all on a path of spiritual evolution and refinement on both sides of the veil. The more we can gain awareness and understanding of the soul's journey while we are here on Earth, the more conscious we will be in the spiritual world. With this consciousness and the awareness that comes with it, we will gain a greater capacity to self-direct and self-correct in a conscious way in the spiritual world. This is a very powerful and important ability.

Now I am going to invite you to read the rest of this chapter to your loved one who has died. If you feel you need to review the steps involved in reading, please feel free to turn to the reading activity in chapter 11, pages 165 through 166. If you would like to, stop for a moment and recall the moods of reverence, tenderness, and gratitude you cultivated in chapter 6. Then come back and begin. Bring your loved one who has died to your mind. Infuse your image of them with feelings of love and a favorite remembrance the two of you shared. Feel them right in front of you. Maybe say a favorite prayer, spiritual poem, or verse that opens your heart further to them. Give to them the image that you would like to share what you are reading with them. Even if you don't feel you have connected with them, trust that you have.

We can begin with some definitions to support you in understanding the soul's journey.

Background Information

The Human Being

Let us look at four aspects of the human being:

The *physical body* has to give way to the laws of the physical Earth, including death and decay.

The *etheric body* is closely related to the plant world and is the home of the life and growth forces that keep the body alive.

The *astral body* is connected to the animal world in the sense that it is driven, via impulses and reactions, by our sympathies (likes) and antipathies (dislikes). When dealing with our astral body, we may feel we lack self-control or willpower, ego or "I consciousness," or self-awareness.

We engage our *ego* to transform our astral, etheric, and physical bodies.

One way to understand these various bodies is with an illustration: If the human being is dead, there is just the physical body. If the human being is sleeping, the physical body and etheric bodies are predominant. When the alarm goes off in the morning, the astral body is either eager to get out of bed or wants to hit the snooze button for another ten minutes of sleep. It is the ego that enables us to climb out of bed, place our two feet on the ground, stand up, and meet the world.

Body-Soul-Spirit

I will let Steiner's words explain this interrelationship: "The spirit is at the center of each human being, and the body is the instrument through which the spirit observes and knows, and also acts in, the physical world. The soul, however, mediates between the two."[2]

Soul Activities: Thinking, Feeling, and Willing

As I mentioned in chapter 14, the soul is made up of the activities of our thinking, feeling, and willing (behavior). One of our tasks is to make our thinking, feeling, and willing aspects more objective in the sense that they are directed by spirit rather than our subjective and personal lower self.

Typically, we are most aware of our thinking. Our feelings can either be numb or at the point of wakening. Our will activities and what lies behind them are the least known and least conscious of these three aspects.

Memory

We don't often stop to think much about our memory, yet it plays an important part in our lives—on both sides of the veil.

Each thought and feeling we have and every act we do creates a memory in our own personal memory treasure chest. The experiences we create through thinking, feeling, and willing in the world are part of the process of individualization; this is what makes us each unique in the world. While living on Earth, we can say that the physical human body helps keep our thinking, feeling, and willing (behavior) "within" our individual selves.

When we recall a memory into our thinking, we typically create a picture or image. Try this now. Pick moments from yesterday that reflect thinking, feeling, and willing or doing: a thought you had about work, a feeling about a loved one, or putting a load of laundry in the washing machine. Did you see pictures of these things in your mind? It is in memories such as these that "we retain in our ego from our experiences in the outer world; in a sense, we bear them with us as the treasure won from experience."[3] If through an accident or illness we lost part of our memory, we would feel that a part of us was missing.

Our memories give us a reference point for who we are. That changes after we die.

Please keep these background points in mind as we move into the general conditions our loved ones will find across the veil.

General Conditions on the Soul's Journey

The Body

Since your loved one no longer has a physical body, they are invisible. For lack of a better analogy, think of them as permeable, like a gas or atmosphere. They no longer have the boundary of their physical skin to separate them from others. Instead, those in the spiritual world interpenetrate or weave through one another. Your loved one will only recognize others, however, if they have had a prior connection to them.

Observing
When they were in a physical body, your loved one had a sense of observing what was outside themselves. In the spiritual world they have a sense of being observed, particularly by the beings of the spiritual hierarchies.

Guidance
Your loved one is being guided or led in the spiritual world by spiritual beings that I like to think of as God's helpers, as well as the angels of the Nine Hierarchies. This guidance takes place through a system of sympathy and antipathy. Sympathy, as you will recall from earlier in the book, is when we have an attraction toward something or someone. Antipathy is a repulsion, a moving away from. Your loved one feels the spiritual beings' approval or disapproval concerning every "deed"—every thought, feeling, and act of will. It is through the wisdom of these spiritual beings that your loved one sees the spiritual essence of their earthly deeds, whether those actions were taken consciously or not. And this continues as your loved one moves into the pure spirit world.

Expanding Out to the Heavens

According to Rudolf Steiner, when we die, we depart the Earth and expand out to the sphere of the Moon. Then we expand further to the spheres of each of the planets and the Sun in this order: Mercury, Venus, Sun, Mars, Jupiter, and Saturn. Then we expand out to the constellations of the zodiac on the periphery: Aries,

Taurus, Gemini, Cancer, Leo, Virgo, Libra, Scorpio, Sagittarius, Capricorn, Aquarius, and Pisces.

An Overview of the Soul's Journey

Here is a summary of the sequence of what Steiner says happens to our loved ones after death, including the planets and constellations that are associated with each stage. *Note:* We can think of these planetary "visits" as both spheres and phases, "sphere" denoting the space between the Earth and said planet and "phase" representing the time period during which we experience what that planet's teachings hold. Of course, time and space are conditions of Earth, but these are the concepts we have to best describe realms that are not of Earth.

- Death: releasing the physical body
- Meeting the guardian at the threshold
- A three-day review process (releasing of the etheric body), connected to memory
- The Moon phase—an intense purification process that takes place during a period of time approximately equal to one-third of your loved one's earthly life
- The Mercury phase
- The Venus phase
- The Sun phase: the Sun is the threshold between the soul world and the pure spirit world
- The Mars phase
- The Jupiter phase
- The Saturn phase
- The zodiac constellations phase
- Silence and rest—the Cosmic Hour

At the Moment of Death— Releasing the Physical Body

At the moment of death the etheric body, astral body, and ego leave the physical body. The physical body is now subject only to the laws of the physical world: death and decay.

Dying is a sacred act. I have been with several people right before they died, but have only been present with three as they took their last breath: my mother, dad, and Lara. Lara was fully conscious as she left her body. My mother and dad were not, though they did vocalize and have facial expressions that reflected their state of being right up to their death. In every case, it was a privilege and honor to witness physical life ending. Each had their own response. My mother spoke of what she was seeing. My dad seemed to be in conversation with a spiritual being, and then there was a clear letting go. I know that Lara was being met by a spiritual being. Perhaps you have had similar experiences of witnessing your loved ones at the moment of death—clues about what they were seeing and experiencing.

I would like to mention at this point that while we on the physical plane may be distressed about our loved one's death, in the spiritual world there is great rejoicing that our loved one has arrived—birthed back into the spiritual world.

At the Threshold of Death

Based of witnessing my loved ones' deaths, I accept the belief that we are taken across the threshold of death by our individual angel of death, which Steiner writes about in *How To Know Higher Worlds*: "I have always stood invisible beside you in the hour of your death."[4]

While I hope that as we cross the threshold, those we love will come to meet us and help us transition over into the spiritual world, I have not found reference to that belief in Rudolf Steiner's writings or lectures. However, he does say that we will meet the Christ, the Lord of Karma, who, throughout the entire time between death and a new birth, will evaluate our deeds and retributions according to the needs of the "general progress of humanity."[5] This supports the reference in the Bible, Acts 10:42, "God has appointed him [the Christ] to judge everyone, alive or dead." I can't think of another spiritual being I would rather have judge my actions than the Christ, the One who loved us so much that he promised: "And know that I am with you always; yes, to the end of time." (Matthew 28:20)

Three Days of Review— Releasing the Etheric Body

After your loved one crosses the threshold, over a period of approximately three days, the etheric body—connected to their memories—is released into the atmosphere around the Earth. After the soul and spirit have left the body at death, the body can no longer assist them in keeping their thinking, feeling, and willing together, so these three aspects will split apart. Their thinking part, including the memories and ego they know themselves to be, "detaches" and a panoramic view of all the memories in their treasure chest, from birth to death, can be seen spreading out horizontally in space in the form of images. These memories are devoid of any attachments to emotion or feeling and are instead seen from a totally objective point of view. Then the images will fade out toward the heavens (cosmic space), taking the ego with them. Because the ego is connected to these memories, your loved one will want to follow them, to find that part of themselves.[6]

The Refinement and Purification Process of the Soul

Releasing the Astral Body

The astral body is the part of the human being that controls behavior through our sympathies (likes) and antipathies (dislikes). As your loved one expands out to the Moon, Mercury, and Venus spheres, they release the astral body through a purification and refinement process. It is during this time period when they have the opportunity to discern the essence of what they learned from their activities during the last incarnation.

The Moon Sphere: Kamaloka—a Purification Period

On Earth, the Moon sphere gives us our creative capacities. After your loved one dies, the Moon sphere is where they feel every action that they did to another. They also experience any unexpressed longings or desires that are still deep within their subconscious and were never expressed. These longings and desires can be filled with pain or joy. This is why it is sometimes labeled as a "purgatory" type of time period, but it can also be seen as a cleansing period and another level of gaining self-knowledge. It is important to note, however, that the soul *wants* this purification.

In *The Spiritual Leadership of Mankind*, Ehrenfried Pfeiffer writes about the spiritual leadership of Saint Francis and one of his tasks after his death: "The first step in his task after death was that once a year, on September 14, he was permitted to go down to Hell (Kamaloka) and gather those souls who had been penetrated by his principles and to bring them, shortening their time, directly to the realm of the Spiritual Sun, the Christ." He further writes, "Rudolf Steiner once said that in a previous incarnation, Francis was one of the most beloved pupils of Buddha."[7]

What are those spiritual qualities? "Each of the twelve original friars exemplified one of the twelve virtues Francis required of his inner, esoteric circle. It is evident that Francis excelled in all twelve of them. They were: faith, simplicity, courtesy, gracious and natural sense, the mind raised in contemplation, virtuous and continual labor, patience, the imitation of Christ, charity, solicitude, humility and fairness."[8] When we penetrate fully into understanding these qualities within our heart and mind, we can pass that wisdom on to our loved ones. We may not be able to change their circumstances, but we can support them in the purification process of the Moon sphere.

How long can your loved one expect to be in the Moon sphere? About a third of the time they were alive. If they were ninety when they died, they would spend thirty years purifying their soul. But if they know these qualities of Saint Francis, it may help shorten that time period and reduce the discomfort they might experience there. It is important to note, however, that the Moon sphere can also contain experiences of joy.

Mercury—Morality

After experiencing the Moon sphere, your loved one expands out to Mercury. On Earth the forces of Mercury give us the capacity to "know thyself," allowing self-assertion of the individual. Some would say it's actually an egotistical part of ourselves, but it can be egotistical in a healthy way because it's how we know who we are. It's how we move through the world.

If while on Earth your loved one cultivated moral integrity about their life and how they lived it, on Mercury they will receive the capacity to work toward the progress of human evolution. Any untruthfulness is addressed in this sphere by working for spirits that cause "hindrances" in the physical world: illness. In the sphere of Mercury there is a sense of working toward the future with a level of social ability, and this works hand in hand with living a moral life on Earth. This is also the time period when they can begin to reconnect with family and friends. This social aspect of Mercury compliments its soul mood color, yellow.

Venus—Spiritual Connections

While on Mercury your loved one finds family and friends, on Venus they will reconnect with those who have the same religious or spiritual beliefs they did. Venus carries the color mood of viridian green and the color mood of sap green.

If on Earth your loved one cultivated spiritual thoughts, tried to understand and penetrate them, and could see the links between the transitory and the eternal, they will attract the cosmic forces of love that Venus holds as a gift for us.

What do *transitory* and *eternal* mean? I love my cowgirl boots, but my boots are temporary; once they wear out, they are not worth anything. This is transitory. When I study spiritual truths, when I try to understand them fully and make them my own, this is essential and lives for eternity. Being conscious in our day-to-day living of what is transitory and what is essential—that is what Venus is all about.

On Earth, we experience the forces of Venus when we express all the loving, devotional qualities of what it is to be human in our best light. "Thou shall love the Lord thy God with all of thy heart, with all of thy soul, with all of thy strength, with all of thy mind and love thy neighbor as thyself." (Mark 12:30–31)

To Summarize What Is Purified

Through the activities that take place in the Moon, Mercury, and Venus spheres, at the end of this period your loved one will have lost their attachments to their last earthly incarnation. One of the vehicles for purification throughout this phase is engaging the two soul activities of sympathy and antipathy.

Recall that sympathy is the force of attraction: an affinity for something that brings us together with that thing or person so its qualities become amplified or take effect. Sympathy is necessary, for it is a tool to remind us that we are part of the whole, part of God.

Antipathy is the opposite: the experience of not liking something or someone. The force here is one of repulsion. With antipathy, boundaries are created or reinforced. Antipathy is necessary because it is a tool to individualize so that we can, *from a place of freedom*, choose to return to God.

Modulating between these two processes allows the human being to become more of who he or she is meant to be: Spirit-Man.

During the release of the astral body, your loved one's soul will have:

- Purified its self-serving desires, those relating to the lowest aspect of bodily life. The fact that they no longer have a physical body to fulfill these desires causes the pain they experience here, which feels like a burning off. (*Note for veil work practice:* A study and understanding of Saint Francis's life's work and qualities is helpful to our loved ones now.)

- Discovered the essential activities and experiences that are important in day-to-day living: those that have a foundation in the spiritual world, the long-lasting, truly important ones that they want to cultivate. Time wasted on things that really don't matter will be illuminated. (*Note for veil work practice:* A conscious reviewing of each day before we sleep is helpful.)

- Learned that it is the spirit that truly endures, no matter how grateful they are for the embodied experience of the physical world. The soul has let go of its attachment to the physical body. Desires and wishes that are purely in one's self-interest are purified because the body is no longer able to fulfill them. This differs from the primal, instinctual desire listed in the first bullet point. Those who have committed suicide have a special challenge with this purification because all their unmet desires remain but their physical body does not. (*Note for veil work practice:* Spiritual reading can provide great comfort, particularly the Gospel of Saint John.)

- Understood the difference between relishing nature and the outdoors on the one hand and understanding the spiritual development of nature on the other. (*Note for veil work practice:*

Striving to understand the spiritual essence of nature and the spiritual process of growing and dying within nature will support your loved ones.)

- Learned that any education they have undertaken for the sole purpose of making life easy for themselves will be reflected back to them, including spiritual education they have explored solely for themselves. They will see the value of educating themselves for the purpose of helping others. (*Note for veil work practice:* Studying biography and understanding the spiritual importance of the different stages of life on Earth are both helpful.)

- Discerned whether they sought experiences for personal pleasure or had a purer motivation. This even applies to such seemingly altruistic activities as working in the arts and sciences. Steiner states that the work of many artists and scientists is rooted in self-interest: motivated by a potential pleasure received. If your loved one's self-interest and pleasure can only be fulfilled in the earthly world, they will feel tethered to the physical body. (*Note:* I do not think Steiner is saying that the spiritual world negates pleasure. Rather, here is an opportunity for your loved one to check in and see if they are creating freely or instead creating conditionally.)

The soul acts as a mediator between the spiritual part of us and our bodies as it travels through these soul worlds. As your loved one purifies their attachments to the physical world, their spirit is learning and growing from the purification of their earthly experience. As their soul becomes more refined, sympathy plays a bigger role. The echoes of the heaviness of the physical are stripped from them, and their soul becomes lighter and moves more freely.

When their spirit has learned as much as it can from that physical incarnation, it knows it is time to shed itself from the soul body and free itself from it, allowing the spirit to move from the more personal soul world to the spirit world where it can continue to learn with a universal, cosmic perspective.

Before they leave the soul world, your loved one will fully realize that they are indeed spiritual beings that used a physical body to fulfill specific tasks while on Earth in their last incarnation. Any remnants of a tendency to the material are burned off, and the spirit is ready to move to what Steiner calls "spirit country" unencumbered. The spirit can only be freed from the soul when the soul has become "at one," in sympathy with the soul world.

Our task as messengers of the spiritual world is to incorporate the spirit into the material world. Only through incarnating in physical bodies can we work in the material world. We must take on physical bodies as our tools so we have something material through which to work on the material world and through which the material world can work on us. However, what works through our human bodily nature is the *spirit*. The intentions and directions for our work in the material world come from the spirit.

The designs for your loved one's work—the intentions and directions for it—come from spirit country (Sun, Mars, Jupiter, Saturn, and the zodiac constellations). Their higher self, their spirit self, develops its own design according to the spiritual laws found in the spirit country. Now, fully separated from its last physical incarnation, the spirit can wander through spirit country, integrating and bringing to maturation all of its learning from previous lifetimes and bringing forward future skills and talents in relationship to what is best for the Earth's evolution from a spiritual perspective. That is the subject of the next chapter.

Veil Work Activity

In your journal write out three things that your loved one will learn or purify in the soul world—the realm of purification of the astral body. Can you identify in your own life how you could start to purify these same three items? Can you find spiritual materials to read that encourage these transformations?

18

The Journey Through Spirit Country: Realm of the Divine

Once in the world of pure spirit, your loved one will finally feel at home. It is here that they will develop goals and intentions for their next life. The landscape is very different in a number of ways from the soul world they left.

As they expand through the various spheres of spirit country (Sun, Mars, Jupiter, and Saturn), they will be met with "celestial music." To the spiritual capacity to "see" that they gained in the soul world, they will add a capacity to "hear" in the spiritual world. Imagine colors sounding out in the form of tones. Everything they meet in the spirit world emits a spiritual radiance.

When I meditate on how beautiful this experience must be, it feels quite overwhelming. Imagine choosing to leave such a blissful place in favor of the trials of life on Earth! Who would want to leave a world that is pure spirit? It gives me an appreciation for each of us who have chosen to reincarnate for the good of human evolution. Surely, we humans, every one of us, are courageous beings striving to become the Tenth Hierarchy of spiritual beings, with an important role and mission, including the furthering of spiritual evolution.

The Sun—Understanding the Other's Faith

The journey continues, expanding out to the center and heart of the cosmos, the Sun, whose soul mood color is radiant white. In the Sun sphere your loved one will start to hear the cosmic symphony. The Sun is about knowing the other. This is why on Earth we want to cultivate an interest in others' religious or spiritual beliefs. If we don't, the repercussion we will experience in the Sun sphere is feeling "every separation, every misunderstanding, every lack of understanding of another person's faith."[1]

It will help us in the Sun sphere if while on Earth we cultivate the thought "In every human breast lies a spark that is divine." We must kindle this spark in ourselves, and we must see it in the other and hold a space for the other to embrace their own spark. The Sanskrit word *namaste* says it beautifully; it means "I bow to the Divine in you."

If we enter the Sun sphere with an understanding of Christ's deed on Earth, in our next incarnation we will receive the gift of vitality. The uniqueness and mystery of Christ's deed is connected to the fact that He is the only spiritual being who left the spiritual world and incarnated into a physical body; He did so for the purpose of bringing Love to the Earth and to all human beings. Thus Christ is connected to Earth until the end of time.

Mars—There Is No Place to Hide

Mars, whose soul mood color is red, is a planet where the cosmic music continues, but it starts to become intermingled with the cosmic word or speech. Mars is strongly connected to our capacity of speech. Steiner says that at first we only hear the cosmic word, but that later we can feel ourselves interwoven with it, becoming part of it. Here your loved one speaks forth their very beingness and reveals themselves to the other. There is no place to hide when you're in the Mars sphere—all is revealed. Speech here is infinitely expressive and creative.

Steiner says that in the seventeenth century Buddha was actually sent to Mars with the task of reducing the materialistic and destructive forces that we find on Earth and replacing them with forces of bravery, courage, enthusiasm, and the energy and capacity for action specifically used to promote peace on Earth.[2]

Jupiter—Wisdom

After your loved one leaves Mars they will expand out even further to Jupiter, whose soul mood color is orange. In the Sun sphere they found the cosmic symphony—music. In the Mars sphere they found the cosmic word. In Jupiter's sphere they enter the realm of cosmic thought.

Here on Earth, this cosmic thought is reflected in wisdom. The qualities that prepare us to be conscious and constructively active in the Jupiter sphere are reverence, devotion, and unity with all of life.

Part of the Earth mission of being human is to individualize while at the same time recognizing that you are connected to all else. You are connected to your neighbor, to the person you work with, to the tree, the mineral, and the starry heavens. You are connected to it all. Mercury helps us with individualizing. The Jupiter sphere reminds us that even though we are individualized, we are also connected with the whole and our actions have ramifications for the whole.

Saturn—Cosmic Memory

Leaving Jupiter, your loved one expands out even further to Saturn, the place of Cosmic Memory. Saturn carries the soul mood of deep indigo. Beredene Jocelyn writes, "Consciousness in the Saturn realm depends on the degree of our *unprejudiced self-knowledge* on earth—not what opinion we had of ourselves, or what others thought of us, but what we are in reality. This implies a cosmic view of ourselves."[3] We all have personal memories, recollections of the events of our lives. Some of us record significant life experiences in journals or diaries, or even write memoirs. Likewise, there is a record of activities on Earth through its evolution. This Cosmic Memory, which some spiritual groups label the Akashic Record, is held by the spiritual beings in the Saturn sphere. In contrast to the word your loved one encounters in the Mars sphere, which is related to the individual human being, the Saturn sphere is filled with the content of the cosmic, universal word out of which everything has been created and will be created, as the prologue of the Gospel of Saint John says:

> In the beginning was the Word:
> the Word was with God
> and the Word was God.
> Through him all things came to be,
> not one thing had its being but through him.

When I think about the Saturn sphere, I cannot help but think of two things Jesus said:

> I tell you on the day of judgment men will render account
> for every careless word that they utter. (Matthew 12:36)

For what I have spoken does not come from myself; no, what I was to say, what I had to speak, was commanded by the Father who sent me, and I know that his commands meant eternal life. And therefore what the Father has told me is what I speak. (John 12:49–50)

The quote from Matthew reminds me of the fact that our careless words are recorded and spiritual beings will be affected by them. The quote from John affirms that the Cosmic Word is the Divine Source out of which all is created.

Thus ends the second phase of your loved one's journey through the planetary spheres. In the first phase—journeying through the Moon, Mercury, and Venus spheres—their soul is refined and purified. As they continue on in the realms of spirit country through the spheres of Mars, Jupiter, and Saturn, their higher self develops.

Zodiac Constellations

After leaving the planetary spheres, your loved one's journey continues on to the perimeter of the zodiac constellations. This area is vast and there is much that takes place there. I am aware that I have likely already presented many concepts about the soul's journey that are new to you. If you want to explore the zodiac spheres further, you may choose to consult the resources at the end of this chapter for more in-depth descriptions. The main thing I want you to know about the zodiac spheres is that this is where the great spiritual beings work on the cosmic ordering of the universe, and it is also the place where "world purposes originate."[4]

Archetypes and the Cosmic Realms

Now I would like to introduce you to the concept of "archetypes" in the sense that Rudolph Steiner perceived them. In the spiritual world, throughout their journey, your loved one will meet the archetypes of the forms of each and every thought that is made manifest in the physical world. Everything manifested on Earth has its origins in these archetypes, which are actually spiritual beings. According to Steiner:

> Archetypes are creative beings, the master builders of everything that comes into existence in the physical and soul worlds. Their forms change quickly, and each archetype has the potential to assume countless specific forms. It is as if the specialized forms well up out of them—one form has hardly been created before its archetype is ready to let the next one pour out. In addition, archetypes do not work alone, but stand in closer or more distant relationship to each other. One archetype may need the help of another to do its creating, and often innumerable archetypes work together so that some particular being can come to life in the soul world or physical world.[5]

Steiner offers an example: if you imagine a painting as existing in the spiritual world before the artist paints it, you will have an image of what is meant by the archetype of the painting.

Beredene Jocelyn decodes Rudolf Steiner's language this way:

> These archetypes are actual beings of the nature of thought, and they are ceaselessly active and assume myriads of forms. In the Mars sphere are the archetypes of everything physical. In the flowing life of the Jupiter realm are the archetypes of all etheric life, forming an harmonious unity. The Sat-

urn region provides the archetypes of soul formations, or the astral world. Beyond the outer planetary spheres is a realm that orders and groups the archetypes of the Mars, Jupiter, and Saturn spheres. Here are the archetypes of human creativity, all original work of the human spirit, all manifestations of genius in any field of life. Beyond this are three more regions which might be designated as the archetypes of the archetypes, the fountainhead for the creative forces, the living germ points, the life kernels and impulses underlying all archetypes. These regions are the highest attainable by man.[6]

There are two ways I have seen this concept at work personally: My painting teacher always told me that we are painting a picture for someone who is coming toward us. I think she was in touch with the knowledge of who that "someone" is: an archetype. Also, in eurythmy, we connect with the poem (poet) or music composition (composer) in the spiritual realm, where it was first given birth—out of an archetype.

As you contemplate your loved one you can consider that wherever they are traveling in the cosmic realms, they are encountering nothing less than the creative forces behind all of existence.

The Cosmic Midnight—and Return to Earth

After your loved one has gone through all of the activities of each of the planetary spheres and zodiac constellations, they rest for a time outside of the perimeter of the zodiac in a state of silence and bliss. They possess the perspective of their past lives, and they hold the possibility of their next incarnation in the future. Now they are at the point of making a decision, one that Rudolf Steiner refers to as the moment of the Cosmic Midnight. This is when your loved one decides either to stay in this place of silence and bliss or reincarnate. A yearning for the freedom that can only be found on Earth calls forth the decision to return, and once that decision is made, your loved one will start to descend back, taking a reverse course through the cosmos, slowly building up the destiny for their next incarnation.

Veil Work Activities

- Draw a diagram of our solar system and the zodiac constellations on a page in your journal. This can be a simple diagram with the names of each planet and constellation, or you can draw images of the planets and constellations as well. Just remember to place the Sun in the center of your paper.

  Now draw a simple diagram of the Soul's Journey. Starting with the Earth, going on to the three-day review, the planets, and expanding out through to the periphery of the zodiac constellations and finally out to the place of Silence. Color the planets using the soul mood color of each to inspire you in noticing the nuances and important aspects of each "stop" on the journey. Note your findings in your journal.

- Review the following table summarizing the gifts and teachings of the planets. Choose one planet per month and explore its gifts and teachings in your life. Note your observations and findings in your journal.

Gifts and Teachings of the Planetary Journey

Planet	Gifts on Earth	Earth Accomplishments	Gifts in the Spiritual World
Moon	Creative capacity	Cultivating purification qualities (like Saint Francis)	Purification
Mercury	I-ness; self-assertion; know thyself	Living a moral life	Working for positive evolution
Venus	Loving, devoted qualities	Discerning the eternal versus the transitory	Cosmic Love
Sun	Life forces (nature, growth, vitality)	Bowing to the Divine in the other	Cosmic Symphony
Mars	Speech	Speech as a creative power	Cosmic Word
Jupiter	Wisdom	Knowledge; reverence (washing of the feet)	Cosmic Thought
Saturn	Capacity for contemplation	Self-knowledge; seeing self from a spiritual perspective	Cosmic Memory/Library; all that has been expressed as the Cosmic Word

Further Reading

Life Beyond Death: Selected Lectures by Rudolf Steiner, Rudolf Steiner Press, 1995.

Theosophy by Rudolf Steiner, Anthrosophic Press, 1994.

From Jesus to Christ by Rudolf Steiner, Rudolf Steiner Press, 1991.

Citizens of the Cosmos by Beredene Jocelyn, SteinerBooks, 1981.

Part 7

Sustaining the Work

If you have been practicing veil work as you read this book, you have traveled far on your journey by now. You have explored setting up a structure for your practice that works best for you, created a journal to capture your experiences, learned the basics of how communicating across the veil often takes place, and opened yourself to co-creative experiences. You have had the opportunity to imagine what life is like in the spiritual world and where your loved one might be in those realms. Even if you have not done much veil work practice and have instead chosen to mainly learn through reading, you have been introduced to a whole new spiritual path, and I hope you feel ready to further apply what you have learned. In this last section of the book, I offer further ideas and inspiration to help you sustain your practice.

19

Supporting Your Practice

Every individual human being is a miniature world. True, he is but a solitary individual in an infinite universe, but no one should underestimate the power or responsibility of an individual.... Though he is only one individual, his presence justifies the existence of all Creation because God values quality, not quantity. Let an entire universe exist only for his benefit, therefore, all so that he can carry out God's will.
—Rabbi Michael L. Munk[1]

When I review the last eighteen years of my work with my daughter and others who have died, I find a common, unifying intention—a personal commitment to:

- being in service to my loved ones in a meaningful and conscious way, and
- holding a sincere desire to lift the veil between them and myself so that our relationships continue to thrive and develop—albeit in a different form from when they were living—allowing for creative collaborations that contribute to spiritual evolution.

You have freedom to choose whether and how you would like to play a part in carrying this work further. This chapter is about supporting you in that effort with ideas for sustaining the work.

Revisiting Commitment and Resistance

The biggest obstacle to sustaining a strong veil work practice is internal resistance. One form of resistance can come about as a result of years of conditioning that tells you it is not "normal" to have a living relationship with those who have died. Another is the idea that if we do veil work, we are holding back our loved ones from where they need to be in the spiritual world; this argument says that our job is to "let them go" and that it is inappropriate to want to be in relationship with them. We can also feel resistance in the form of judgment: thinking that we are not doing enough, that we are not doing it right, or that we are not being effective because we are not receiving the kind of response we expect.

All of these sources of resistance—which can even take place on an unconscious level, making them more difficult to address—can show up in our lives in the form of missing our planned reading sessions. Some of us are naturally graced with resiliency and tenacity and we can "right the ship" as soon as we realize we are not following through on our commitment as we intended. And sometimes we need to meet that resistance through recommitting. Here are some guidelines that will help you do just that.

Rhythm + Faith = Commitment

If you need to refresh your commitment, I encourage you to go back to chapter 5 and review the sections on a consistent rhythm (page 64) and faith (page 67). The formula "rhythm + faith = commitment" is your friend. As that chapter also explains, a steady rhythm of practice at the same time each day will develop into a habit, and once your veil work practice has become a habit, it will be much more difficult for your resistance to have the final word!

As well, keep in mind that on those days when life events prevent you from reinforcing your habit of veil work at a regular time, a less formal practice consisting of carrying your loved ones with you into other parts of your daily activities counts too. And you will enjoy your connection to your loved ones just as much.

Revisit the Structure of Your Practice

I am going to send you back to chapter 5 one more time because it offers a way to make it easier to keep the rhythm of your practice going. Structuring for Success on pages 69 and 70 offers ideas that have worked for me for overcoming resistance. However, self-knowledge is the key to establishing the most supportive structure for you, so if you are "falling out of the habit" of doing regular veil work, take another look at the structure you have set in place and see if you can find ways to make your practice more inviting—and exciting!

Be Open to New Ways to Connect

Veil work is so satisfying to me that I am always on the lookout for ways to bring my loved ones into my daily life, almost no matter what I'm doing. I encourage you to develop a quality of curiosity about what other ways may be available to you, asking yourself, "What can I do today (or during this hour, or at this moment) that would allow me to reconnect with my loved ones outside of my formal veil work practice?" Here are some ways I do that. I offer them to spark your imagination.

- Integrate veil work with your professional work. Many of us are blessed that our work is spiritual in nature, or has spiritual components to it. When I am working on a project of a spiritual nature, I can find myself reading related materials for hours, sometimes more than three or four hours a day. Being conscious of my loved one's presence during that time is important. Plus, there is a side benefit: often, they help lead me to answers I am seeking—and suddenly we are co-creating together.

- I have an inner knowing that I can also read spiritual materials for five minutes and still develop and maintain a connection. I can even have one spiritual thought that brings my loved ones close.

- I brought Lara and my loved ones into my days throughout all my years of eurythmy training. I envisioned them by my side during classes, practices, and performances.

- I did the same with my color studies, bringing my loved ones into my reading about the spiritual nature of color, color exercises, and paintings, as well as bringing them imaginations of color: those found in nature including sunrises, sunsets, rainbows, and cloud formations.

- I bring my loved ones in during my piano lessons and practice sessions. Classical music has a lawfulness that is attractive and spiritually nourishing. If you don't play a musical instrument now, you might find yourself being *led* to learning how to play one.

- I bring them to live classical music concerts, filling myself with music and lifting that experience to my loved ones.

- I bring them in when I sing spiritual music. Singing with others, choral singing, adds a whole other dimension to this gift of music.

- When I am working in my garden, I share through imaginations the growth patterns of nature: the spiraling nature of rose petals, for example, and the green star that is formed on the underside of the blossom.

- When I come home late, as I walk into my home I look up to the starry heavens and blow Lara a kiss. I look for planets and constellations that are in my line of sight. I think of how when I fall asleep that night, I will expand out to the heavens and actually be able to connect with her while I sleep.

- When I am hiking in nature, I bring my loved ones along and hold thoughts of the progression of the cycle of the seasons, the forces of growth and decay within them, and the nature spirits that are hard at work.

- I make the eurythmy gesture of O (page 221). I gather into this gesture the most devoted love I can offer my daughter, placing her right in the center of my O, knowing that I offer her this gesture in complete freedom, both hers and mine. I also practice receiving an O gesture from my mother or father. Both the giving and receiving are quite powerful.

- When I'm in my kitchen, I will often do a random eurythmy gesture (I-A-O) and offer it to my loved one. (See instructions on pages 218 to 221.)

- While I'm doing the dishes, I might send my daughter the color magenta with the accompanying words: "I love you. I still miss the physical you."

- I use the essential oils that were used in Jesus's time to support my reading from the Bible or Steiner's books, which offer an esoteric look at the teachings of the Bible. Inhaling fragrances like spikenard, frankincense, and myrrh while reading invokes a feeling of that time period. I have also experimented with these oils at other times, applying them to my wrists or near my nose. I can report one experience when I used frankincense and upon waking had the knowing that my grandmother on my dad's side of the family was there at the foot of my bed. My sense of her presence was that she was indicating her help and guidance on a project that I was working on.

- I practice seeing, feeling, and observing conversations with my loved ones or messages from them.

- "When two or more are gathered." I once participated in a book study group dedicated to reading to those who have died, a monthly event. Sometimes there were only two of us, and at other times there were five or six. Veil work is so often solo work, and it was wonderful to share this practice with others. (Please see page 260 for more.)

Self-Care

As with life in general, when you do veil work it is important to place a priority on your own personal self-care. What that looks like is different for each of us, but throughout your day you might want to enjoy a refreshing walk, eat nourishing foods, get plenty of sleep, and generally treat yourself with the same intentional love and care you feel for and give to your loved one.

Creating Boundaries

What happens when you feel overwhelmed by the work and then feel guilty because you miss a session? What do you do if someone other than the primary person you are building a relationship with wants a connection with you? *Before* these things happen, I suggest you prepare for having too many impulses coming toward you by establishing some boundaries.

In creating boundaries we are working with the soul quality of antipathy, which, as you learned earlier in the book, can be a powerful spiritual force that creates separation. As I mentioned in chapter 17 on the soul's journey, this is an important quality in the individualization process.

Having clear boundaries is essential to this work—and for a healthy life in general. If you are not familiar with how to create boundaries, or you find yourself always saying yes and then wishing you had said no, I highly recommend Drs. Henry Cloud and John Townsend's book *Boundaries: When to Say Yes, How to Say No to Take Control of Your Life*. The authors define the different types of boundaries you can establish, including spiritual boundaries, and devote an entire chapter to the ten laws of boundaries. The authors write from a classic Christian perspective, which means that at times it is a little too conservative for me, but I have learned to glean the pearls of wisdom from their work to create my own template for setting boundaries.

Boundaries are an individual matter, and it is important that you find your own answers here, but let me tell you what I have done in the situations I mentioned.

Feeling Guilty About Being Overwhelmed with the Work and Missing a Session

Sometimes I feel overly responsible for this work. When this happens, I remember the message of the quote that opens this chapter. I am reminded that, yes, there is a responsibility to meet, *but* God and my loved ones are more interested in the quality of the work I do.

I also make sure that I am doing veil work in love and with joy—or I do not do it. Exhaustion lacks both love and joy, so refraining from this work when I am overly tired is one of my boundaries.

Someone Else Who Has Died Wants to Connect with You

I have in freedom invited many members of my family and loved ones to join me in my reading. I have also had miscellaneous requests from others to read to them. I have generally tried to honor their requests. However, when I decided to enter eurythmy training full time, I consciously invited them to join me at class—and at the same time advised them that I could not read any materials not related to my training. I felt that they completely honored that request; I literally felt a sense of lightness in response.

I have never felt threatened or pressured to be in relationship with someone who has died. I think the key to this work is to focus on *loved* ones who have died. I know they have my best interest in mind and that the overall intention of our work together is to serve God and further spiritual evolution for the good of all. If you experience anything that feels like pressure or that feels unhealthy in any way, immediately end that relationship. Then call in your guardian angel. For me, I would also call in the Christ and the Archangel Michael and ask for their help in severing that connection immediately.

Start a Wonders at the Veil Study Group

A great way to sustain your veil work practice is to join with others and share your experience, so support your practice by starting a book study group. The meetings can be held at your home, or if that is not comfortable for you, local libraries often offer rooms at no charge. Check your local bookshop and library for suggestions on building a successful reading group. Here are two approaches that I have found useful, and these principles will be familiar because they are the same as what works for veil work: establish a consistent rhythm, and create a group intention so you always have that as your touchstone.

Veil Work Activities

Now it is time for your last veil work activities. Congratulations on reaching this milestone!

- If you have not already done so, go back and review your initial intention. Read it again and see if you want to change it in any way. If you do, write your new intention on a fresh page in your journal.

- Think about whether or not you would enjoy starting a *Wonders at the Veil* study group. If you decide you would, do not hesitate—start with one friend. If the friend does not live nearby, you can use Skype to meet. Give that person a call now and see if they are interested in taking up this spiritual practice with you.

Your Last Eurythmy Exercise

Do one more eurythmy exercise, this one as you recite a verse written by Rudolf Steiner. This practice is very nourishing and strengthening.

Stand upright with your feet together, your arms and hands placed at your sides, your head slightly lowered. Knees are soft. Note where the weight of your body is on the bottoms of your feet—heels, toes, or on the balls of your feet. Place your weight on the balls of your feet and start your movement and reciting from there.

Steadfast I stand in the world. (Place your left foot out to your left about six inches.)

With Certainty I tread the path of life. (Place your right foot out to your right about six inches.)

Love I cherish in the depth of my being. (Your left hand comes up to your heart (sternum) and then extends out to the left at heart level. Your gaze follows your arm movement to the left.)

Hope I place in all my deeds. (Your right hand comes up to your heart (sternum) and then extends out to the right at heart level. Your gaze follows your arm movement to the right.)

Confidence I impress into my thinking. (Raise your head upright. Your gaze is now forward, looking straight ahead.)

These five give me life.

These five lead me to my goals.

(After the last sentence, bring your right hand to your heart, your left hand to your heart. Bring your right foot six inches to the left and your left foot six inches to the right. You are now standing with your feet together and hands at your heart.)

Feel all the qualities being consolidated into your heart center: steadfastness, certainty, love, hope, and confidence. Wait for a moment. Release your hands and place your arms at your sides. Wait another moment in silence.

20

In Closing

Dear Friend,

As our work together comes to a close, I would like for us to revisit Albert Steffen's words:

> Human freedom may choose whether or not to seek and maintain a conscious relationship with the dead. Nothing, either from within or from without, compels it. It is a deed of purest love.[1]

I do this work because I love my daughter and the others I am in touch with who have crossed the threshold. I believe in our ongoing connection and care for each other throughout eternity. Your veil work practice will also be rooted in loving connection, and there is tremendous power in that.

You have already started to lift the veil between yourself and your loved ones simply by reading this book. In a world where we have been told that we are to leave the dead alone, you have shown that you are open to another possibility. And I am grateful for that.

Throughout your reading, your thoughts have turned to the spiritual, your heart has been warmed, and you have acted for the good of all. Even if you do not start a veil work practice and just reading this book is all you are able to do for now, you have planted a seed for the future. This is a seed you may choose to nurture later in this lifetime, or you and your loved ones may cultivate it in future lifetimes. If you do decide to fully embrace veil work now—and I hope and trust that many readers will—I look forward to hearing from you about what your research reveals.

Be steadfast. Know that you might sometimes fail, but keep trying. Your work at the threshold is very important. Know that when you "hear" from your loved one, the messages will be filled with warmth and love, and that they will always leave you the space to come to this work in a state of freedom.

Remember: now is the time in our spiritual evolution to create conscious, *living* relationships with loved ones who have died. I welcome you to this sacred, heart-opening work.

With love and respect,

Lynn

Institute for Veil Work

Veil work is the spiritual practice of approaching the veil between the physical and spiritual worlds with the specific intention to be of service to our loved ones who have died and to remain in a living relationship with them, which may include co-creating with them.

The Institute for Veil Work:
- Educates people on what veil work is and why now is the time to take up this spiritual practice
- Inspires people to engage with the spiritual practices of veil work
- Affirms co-creative deeds that cultivate the virtues of Truth and Beauty and acts of Goodness in the world
- Collects research and resources in order to connect individuals who are actively doing, or interested in doing, veil work

For more information and to get the most current updates go to: InstituteforVeilWork.org.

Acknowledgments

udolf Steiner, I am eternally grateful. Your work on how to serve those who have died changed my life.

Butch Stull, I am grateful for our shared parenting of our extraordinary daughter.

My loved ones who have died: Woo hoo! We did it! Thank you for the inspiration, guidance, and will forces you shared in co-creating this book.

Sheridan McCarthy of Meadowlark Publishing Services (larkonline.net), thank you for the professional and personal skills you brought to shaping the contents of this book and the important stories I wanted to share within it. You are amazing! Thanks also to you and your partner, Stanton Nelson, for making the end result look beautiful. Nikki Van De Car of KN Literary Arts, thank you for connecting me with Sheridan.

Gene Gollogly of Anthroposophic Press and SteinerBooks, thank you for generously granting me reprint permissions.

Shannon Jackson Arnold, thank you for being the Earth Angel for this book. Your consistent love, encouragement, and professional input to this body of work are deeply appreciated.

Linda Connell, thank you for your care in reading and editing this book from two perspectives: as an Anthroposophist and as a friend.

Mary Ruud, thank you for proofing the chapter on eurythmy. You inspire me.

Eileen Petzold, thank you for your never-ending love, feedback, and being "there" for me. You are the best sister. Ever.

Rick Rollins and David Rollins, how did I get so blessed as to have you two as brothers? Thanks for letting me include you both in this book and for all your loving support.

Donna Hickey, I can still remember the moment you and Lara saw each other. Thank you for loving us the way you do and for letting me share the "dream" of you and Lara.

Rev. Cynthia Hindes (thechristiancommunity.org) and Jeremy Smith (anthropopper.wordpress.com), thank you both for giving me permission to reference your blog posts.

Carolyn Bottum, thank you for your permission to cite your father, Bill Bottum's, work.

Mary Stewart Adams, you rock. Thanks for the quote, and for your advocacy for dark skies (midarkskypark.org).

Kim Lane, Sylvie Richard, Carol Ann Williamson, Shannon Jackson Arnold, Linda Connell, and Amie Slate, thank you for sharing with me your experiences of working with those who have died. I value that you each know how important this work is.

Truus Geraets, thank you for your eurythmy instruction, gentle nudges, and support. You were instrumental in changing the course of my life.

Kanako Seki, thank you for speaking what you heard.

Kim Tedford, thank you. I know that you know how important this work is to me.

Peggy Carson, thank you for your love for Lara.

Sheila James, thank you for your love and support for my creative endeavors.

Lynn Kitchen, thank you for your unconditional friendship and love.

Dan Switalski, thank you for bringing joy into my life. At just the right time.

Feeling grateful and blessed,
Lynn Rollins Stull

Notes

Chapter 1

1. Rudolf Steiner, *Life Between Death and Rebirth*, tr. R. M. Querido. Spring Valley, NY: Anthroposophic Press, 1968, 169.
2. Barbara Marx Hubbard, *The Revelation: Our Crisis Is a Birth*. Santa Barbara, CA: The Foundation for Conscious Evolution, 1993, 13.
3. Pew Research Center, "Many Americans Mix Multiple Faiths." http://www.pewforum.org/2009/12/09/many-americans-mix-multiple-faiths/.
4. Rudolf Steiner, *How to Know Higher Worlds*, tr. Christopher Banford. Hudson, NY: Anthroposophic Press, 1994, 109.
5. Mircea Eliade et al, ed., *The Encyclopedia of Religion*. New York: Macmillan, 1995, 415–16.
6. "The affairs of the living and dead—Our African ancestors." South Africa. http://www.southafrica.net/za/en/articles/entry/article-southafrica.net-our-african-ancestors. Retrieved 3/15/16.
7. "Veneration of the Dead." Wikipedia. https://en.wikipedia.org/wiki/Veneration_of_the_dead. Retrieved 3/1/16.
8. "Prayers for the Dead." http://www.catholic.com/encyclopedia/prayers-for-the-dead. Retrieved 3/1/16.

Chapter 2

1. Rudolf Steiner, "The Spiritual Communion of Mankind." http://wn.rsarchive.org/Lectures/19221223p01.html.
2. Pew Research Center, "Many Americans Mix Multiple Faiths.," http://www.pewforum.org/2009/12/09/many-americans-mix-multiple-faiths/.

3. His Holiness the Dalai Lama, "Reincarnation." http://www.dalailama. com/messages/statement-of-his-holiness-the-fourteenth-dalai-lama-tenzin-gyatso-on-the-issue-of-his-reincarnation.

4. Mohandas K. Gandhi, *Young India*, April 2, 1931. Quoted in Louis Fischer, ed., *The Essential Gandhi*. New York: Vintage, 2002, 269.

5. Gary Varner, *Ghosts, Spirits & the Afterlife in Native American Folklore and Religion*. Lulu, 2010.

6. Rudolf Steiner, *The Gospel of St. Luke*, 3rd edition, 3rd printing. Forest Row, E. Sussex, UK: Rudolf Steiner Press, 1988, 183–4.

7. Past Forward, "Henry Ford and Reincarnation." http://blog.thehenryford.org/2015/08/henry-ford-and-reincarnation/.

8. "Reincarnation—Famous People." http://reincarnation.ws/famous_people/.

9. "Pythagoras." *Stanford Encyclopedia of Philosophy*. http://plato.stanford.edu/entries/pythagoras/. Retrieved 02/16/16.

10. AZ Quotes. http://www.azquotes.com/quote/603795.

11. "Reincarnation—Famous People." http://reincarnation.ws/famous_people/.

12. Andy Jackson, "General George Patton And Reincarnation." Psychics Directory Articles. http://www.psychicsdirectory.com/articles/general-george-patton-and-reincarnation/.

13. Wordsworth: "Ode: Intimations of Immortality from Recollections of Early Childhood," 1804.

14. The Electric Ben Franklin, "Benjamin Franklin's Funeral and Grave." http://www.ushistory.org/franklin/philadelphia/grave.htm.

Chapter 3

1. Carlos Castaneda, *The Active Side of Infinity* (New York: Harper) 1999, 10. In Wayne Dyer, *The Power of Intention* (New York: Hay House) 2005, 4.

2. Dyer, *The Power of Intention*.

3. Ibid., 12.

4. Ibid.

Chapter 4

1. Rudolf Steiner, *Staying Connected: How to Continue Your Relationships with Those Who Have Died*. Great Barrington, MA: Anthroposophic Press, 1999, 33.

Chapter 5

1. Will Durant, *The Story of Philosophy: The Lives and Opinions of the World's Greatest Philosophers*. New York: Pocket Books, 1952, 76.
2. Stephen Covey, *The 7 Habits of Highly Effective People: Restoring the Character Ethic*. New York: Free Press, 47.
3. Rev. Cynthia Hindes, "Guardian Angels." The Christian Community: Movement for Religious Revival. http://www.thechristiancommunity. org/features/essays-and-articles/guardian-angels/. Retrieved 2/11/16.
4. Christian Morgenstern, "An Angel Speaks," Cindy Hindes, tr. In Hindes, "Guardian Angels."
5. Jeremy Smith, "Rudolf Steiner & Angels—The Current Work of the Angels within Human Beings." Anthropopper, September 28, 2015. https://anthropopper.wordpress.com/2015/09/; http://en.gravatar.com/ jeremysmith33. Retrieved 2/11/16.

Chapter 6

1. Rudolf Steiner, lecture, "The Mission of Reverence." In *Metamorphoses of the Soul: Paths of Experience*, vol. 1. London: Rudolf Steiner Press, 1983.
2. Rudolf Steiner, *Eurythmy: Its Birth and Development*. Trobridge, Wilts, UK: Anatasi Ltd, Cromwell Press, 2002, 41.
3. Rudolf Steiner, *Eurythmy as Visible Speech*. Weobley, Herefordshire, UK: Anastasi Ltd., 2005, 67.
4. Ibid., 71.

Chapter 7

1. National Institute on Drug Abuse, "Popping Pills: Prescription Drug Abuse in America." http://www.drugabuse.gov/related-topics/ trends-statistics/infographics/popping-pills-prescription-drug-abuse- in-america. Retrieved 2/18/16.

2. Walter Isaacson, *Einstein: His Life and Universe*. New York: Simon & Schuster, 2007, 9.

3. Marc J. Seifer, *Wizard: The Life and Times of Nikola Tesla—Biography of a Genius*. New York: Citadel Press, 1998, 11.

4. Temple Grandin, *Thinking in Pictures: My Life with Autism*. New York: Vintage Books, 2006, 3.

5. Stuart Wilde, *Sixth Sense: Including the Secrets of the Etheric Subtle Body*. Carlsbad, CA: Hay House, 21.

6. Albert Steffen, *Meetings With Rudolf Steiner*. Dornach, Switzerland: Verlag fur Schöne Wissenschaften, 1961, 106–7.

Chapter 8
1. Steiner, *Staying Connected*, 174.

2. Stuart Wilde, *Affirmations by Stuart Wilde*. Carlsbad, CA: Hay House, 1987, 5.

3. Steiner, *Staying Connected*, 188.

4. Ibid., 157.

5. Kelly Connor, *To Cause a Death: The Aftermath of an Accidental Killing*. West Hoathly, W. Sussex, UK: Clairview Books, 2004.

Chapter 9
1. Steiner, *Life Between Death and Rebirth*.

Chapter 10
1. Steiner, *Staying Connected*, 29.

2. Rudolf Steiner, *Life Beyond Death*. London: Rudolf Steiner Press, 1995.

3. Liane Collot d'Herbois, *Light, Darkness and Colour in Painting Therapy*. Edinburgh: Floris Books, 2000.

4. *The Jerusalem Bible*. London: Darton, Longman & Todd and New York: Doubleday, 1966.

5. Rudolf Steiner, *Angels: Selected Lectures*. Forest Row, E. Sussex, UK: Rudolf Steiner Press, 1996.

6. Rudolf Steiner, *Spiritual Beings in the Heavenly Bodies and in the Kingdoms of Nature*. Hudson, NY: Anthroposophic Press, 1992.

7. Rudolf Steiner, *The Spiritual Hierarchies and the Physical World: Zodiac, Planets & Cosmos*. Hudson, NY: SteinerBooks, 1996.

8. Gina Cerminara, *Many Mansions: The Edgar Cayce Story on Reincarnation*. New York: Signet, 1988.

9. Brian L. Weiss, *Many Lives, Many Masters: The True Story of a Prominent Psychiatrist, His Young Patient, and the Past-Life Therapy That Changed Both Their Lives*. New York: Simon and Schuster, 1988.

10. Rudolf Steiner, *Karmic Relationships: Esoteric Studies*. Forest Row, E. Sussex, UK: Rudolf Steiner Press, first edition 1973, reprinted 2002.

11. Rudolf Steiner, *Manifestations of Karma*. London: Rudolf Steiner Press, 1996.

12. Carson-Dellosa Publishing, *Religions of the World* (Peter Bedrick Young People's Encyclopedia series). New York: Peter Bedrick, 2000.

13. Ra Uru Hu and Lynda Bunnell, *Human Design: The Definitive Book of Human Design, The Science of Differentiation*. Carlsbad, CA: HDC Publishing, 2011.

14. Richard Rudd, *Gene Keys: Unlocking the Higher Purpose Hidden in Your DNA*. London: Watkins Publishing, 2013.

15. "Sakena Yacoobi Wins Opus Prize, $1,000,000, For Founding The Afghan Institute Of Learning." http://www.huffingtonpost.com/2013/11/14/sakena-yacoobi-opus-prize_n_4277015.html.

16. The Pema Chödrön Foundation, http://pemachodronfoundation.org. Retrieved 3/15/16.

17. Malala Yousafzai, *I Am Malala*. Boston: Back Bay Books, 2013, 129.

18. Ehrenfried Pfeiffer, *The Spiritual Leadership of Mankind*. Spring Valley, NY: Mercury Press, 1985, 17.

19. Rudolf Steiner, April 27, 1913, Düsseldorf, Germany, in Steiner, *Staying Connected*, 56.

20. Steiner, *Life Between Death and Rebirth*.

21. Dore Deverell, *Light Beyond The Darkness: The Healing of a Suicide Across the Threshold of Death*. Forest Row, E. Sussex, UK: Temple Lodge, 1989.

Chapter 11

1. Wassily Kandinsky, *Concerning the Spiritual in Art*. New York: Dover, 1977 (first published 1912).

2. Brain Pickings, "Kandinsky on the Spiritual Element in Art and the Three Responsibilities of Artists." https://www.brainpickings.org/2014/06/02/kandinsky-concerning-the-spiritual-in-art/. Retrieved 3/1/16.

3. John O'Donohue, *Divine Beauty: The Invisible Embrace*. New York: Bantam, 2003.

4. Patrick Kavanaugh, *Spiritual Lives of the Great Composers*. Grand Rapids, MI: Zondervam 1966.

5. Armin J. Husemann, *Human Hearing and the Reality of Music*. Great Barrington, MA: SteinerBooks, 2012.

6. Michael Chekhov, *The Path of the Actor*. New York: Routledge, 2005; *Lessons for the Professional Actor*. New York: PAJ Publications, 2001.

7. M. C. Richards, *Centering in Pottery, Poetry, and the Person*. Middletown, CT: Wesleyan University Press, 1989, 94.

8. Margaret Bennel and Isabel Wyatt, *Shakespeare's Flowering of the Spirit*. Great Barrington , MA: SteinerBooks, 2008.

9. Susan Raven, *Nature Spirits: The Remembrance*. Forest Row, E. Sussex, UK: Clairview Books, 2013.

10. Rudolf Steiner Archive, "The Agricultural Course." http://wn.rsarchive.org/Biodynamics/GA327/English/BDA1958/Ag1958_index.html. Retrieved 2/11/16.

11. Wendell Berry, *The Unsettling of America: Culture and Agriculture*. Berkeley, CA: Counterpoint Press, 1996.

12. Willi Sucher, *Cosmic Christianity & the Changing Countenance of Cosmology: An Introduction to Astrosophy: A New Wisdom of the Stars*. Great Barrington, MA: SteinerBooks, 1993.

13. Norman Davidson, *Sky Phenomena: A Guide to Naked-Eye Observation of the Stars*. Great Barrington, MA: Lindisfarne Press, 2001.

14. Institute of Noetic Sciences, "What Are the Noetic Sciences?" http://www.noetic.org/about/what-are-noetic-sciences. Retrieved 2/11/16.

15. StarTeach Astronomy Education, "The Astronomy of the Mayans." http://www.starteachastronomy.com/mayan.html. Retrieved 2/11/16.

16. "About Bill Bottum," Within Your Reach: The Beatitudes in Business and Everyday Life. https://billbottum.wordpress.com/about-bill-bottum/. Retrieved 2/11/16.

17. Dorothy L. Lenz, George SanFacon, and Larry C. Spears, editors. *Within Your Reach: The Beatitudes in Business and Everyday Life*. http://www.spearscenter.org/docs2010/WithinYourReachBillBottum2010.pdf. Retrieved 2/11/16.
18. Ibrahim Abouleish and Markus Kirchgessner, *Sekem: A Sustainable Community in the Egyptian Desert*. Edinburgh: Floris Books,2005.
19. Martin Large, *Common Wealth: For a Free, Equal, Mutual, and Sustainable Society*. Stroud, Glos, UK: Hawthorn Press, 2010.

Chapter 12
1. Steiner, *Staying Connected*, chapter 7.

Chapter 13
1. Howard Gardner, *Truth, Beauty, and Goodness Reframed: Educating for the Virtues in the Age of Truthiness and Twitter*. New York: Basic Books, 2012, ix–x.
2. Steve McIntosh, *Integral Consciousness and the Future of Evolution*. St. Paul, MN: Paragon House, 2007.
3. Rudolf Steiner, "Truth, Beauty and Goodness," lecture January 19, 1923. http://wn.rsarchive.org/Lectures/19230119p01.html#sthash.yzCt21J6.dpu, 15. Retrieved 2/11/16.

Chapter 14
1. Kandinsky, *Concerning The Spiritual in Art*. Boston: MFA Publications, 2006, 106–7.

Chapter 15
1. Collot d'Herbois, *Light, Darkness and Colour in Painting Therapy*, 250.
2. Rudolf Steiner, *Colour*, second ed. Forest Row, E. Sussex, UK: Rudolf Steiner Press, 1992.
3. Ibid., 200.

Chapter 16
1. Marjorie Raffe, Cecil Harwood, and Marguerite Lundgren, *Eurythmy and the Impulse of Dance*. London: Rudolf Steiner Press, 2014, 26.

2. Rudolf Steiner, *The Presence of the Dead*. Hudson, NY: Anthroposophic Press, 1990, 24.

3. Steffen, *Meetings With Rudolf Steiner*, 113.

4. Magdalene Siegloch, *How the New Art of Eurythmy Began*. Forest Row, E. Sussex, UK: Temple Lodge Publishing, 1997, 11.

5. Ibid., 13.

6. Raffe, Harwood, and Lundgren, *Eurythmy and the Impulse of Dance*, 14.

7. Rudd, *Gene Keys*, 501.

8. Goswami Kriyananda, *A Yoga Dictionary of Basic Sanskrit Terms*. Chicago: The Temple of Kriya Yoga, 1996, 46.

9. Swami Krishnananda, tr. *The Mandukya Upanishad*. Rishikesh, India: The Divine Life Society, 1996, ebook, 10.

10. "John 1:14 in Hebrew." http://www.hebrew-streams.org/works/ntstudies/divrei-yishkon.html. Retrieved 3/21/16.

11. John 1:1–3. *The Jerusalem Bible, New Testament*. New York: Doubleday, 1966, 146.

12. Rabbi Michael L. Munk, *The Wisdom in the Hebrew Alphabet*. New York: Mesorah Publications, 2012, 43.

13. David Sacks, *Letter Perfect: The Marvelous History of Our Alphabet from A to Z*. New York: Broadway Books, 2003, 52.

14. Rudolf Steiner, *Eurythmy as Visible Singing*. Dornach, Switzerland, Rudolf Steiner-Nachlassverwaltung, 1975, 6.

15. Rudolf Steiner, *Eurythmy as Visible Speech*. Dornach, Switzerland: Rudolf Steiner-Nachlafverwaltung, 1982, 34–35.

16. Rudolf Steiner, *The Influence of the Dead on Destiny*. Great Barrington, MA: Steiner Books, 2007, 58–59.

17. Steiner, lecture, August 26, 1923, in *Eurythmy as Visible Speech*. Weobley, Herefordshire, UK: Anastasi Ltd., 2005, 181.

Chapter 17

1. Mary Stewart Adams, program director and resident stargazer, Headlands International Dark Sky Park, May 12, 2015.

2. Rudolf Steiner, *Theosophy: An Introduction to the Supersensible Knowledge of the World and the Destination of Man*. Hudson, NY: Anthroposophic Press, 1994, 109.

3. Steiner, *Life Beyond Death*, 38.
4. Steiner, *How to Know Higher Worlds*, 188.
5. Rudolf Steiner, Lecture 10. *From Jesus to Christ*. Forest Row, E. Sussex, UK: Rudolf Steiner Press, 1991, 171.
6. Rudolf Steiner, "Metamorphosis of the Memory of Life After Death," lecture. In *Life Beyond Death*. London: Rudolf Steiner Press, 1995, 40–41.
7. Pfeiffer, *The Spiritual Leadership of Mankind*, 22.
8. Ibid., 23.

Chapter 18
1. Steiner, *Between Death and Rebirth*. London: Rudolf Steiner Press, 1975, 43.
2. Rudolf Steiner, *The Secret Stream: Christian Rosenkreutz and Rosicrucianism*, lectures. Hudson, NY: Anthroposophic Press, 2000, 150–51.
3. Beredene Jocelyn, *Citizens of the Cosmos: Life's Unfolding from Conception through Death to Rebirth*. Great Barrington, MA: SteinerBooks, 2009, 167.
4. Ibid., 168.
5. Steiner, *Theosophy*, 124–5.
6. Jocelyn, *Citizens of the Cosmos*, 168.

Chapter 19
1. Munk, *The Wisdom in the Hebrew Alphabet*, 24.

Chapter 20
1. Steffen, *Meetings With Rudolf Steiner*, 101.

About The Author

*L*ynn Rollins Stull is the director of the Institute for Veil Work and founder of Arts2Thrive, a creative arts practice helping professionals and teams form better connections through art and eurythmy movement. She is also creator of Easing Grief, a video home study program designed to empower, educate, and support those who are interested in deepening their connection with their loved ones who have died. Lynn's veil work journey began in 1997 after her daughter, Lara, died. Her practice of co-creating through the veil with Lara and other loved ones has led her on a path to becoming an award-winning artist and professional eurythmist.

CPSIA information can be obtained
at www.ICGtesting.com
Printed in the USA
BVHW081926050819
555087BV00001B/76/P